"I am grateful for all the gems this book offers. ꟷ
supports that Joe shares light the way towards ꞇ
cultivating relational learning communities which is wɥɑʇ ᴜᴜ.
perhaps our lovely world, need now more than ever!"

—*Michelle Stowe, Director of Connect RP*

"Joe brings a personal and authentic vulnerability, along with a wealth of knowledge and experience to school practices that remain more critical than ever before."

—*Eric Rossen, PhD, NCSP, Director, Professional Development and Standards, National Association of School Psychologists*

"The combination of practical and applicable practices grounded in research is what is needed to move forward in becoming a restorative and trauma-informed school!"

—*Mathew Portell, Principal of Fall Hamilton Elementary School and Founder of the Trauma-Informed Educators Network*

"This book is a MUST HAVE for anyone serving children in an education institution. Thank you, Joe, for your courage, your vulnerability, and your deep knowledge of students."

—*Melissa Sadin, EdD, MEd, MAT, Ducks & Lions: Trauma Sensitive Resources, www.traumasensitive.com*

"Brummer gives educators a large toolbox from which to draw numerous practices that build positive relationships and create emotionally safe classrooms. If this book doesn't change educators' mindsets about how to best support struggling students, I don't know what will."

—*Martha A. Brown, author of* Creating Restorative Schools: Setting Schools Up to Succeed

"This book is coming out at the perfect time. The world is beginning to understand what is needed to help our students and schools heal. It is an easy-to-read guide explaining the why and then giving the reader the skills to do the what."

—*Dennis Littky, Co-founder and Co-director of The Met School, Co-founder of Big Picture Learning and Founder and President of College Unbound*

"This book goes beyond a process for restorative justice and teaches you how to create safe spaces for every learner."

—*Shatanna DeRosie, Assistant Principal, Windsor High School*

BUILDING A TRAUMA-INFORMED RESTORATIVE SCHOOL

Skills and Approaches for Improving
Culture and Behavior

JOE BRUMMER
with
MARGARET THORSBORNE

Foreword by Judy Atkinson

Jessica Kingsley Publishers
London and Philadelphia

First published in Great Britain in 2021 by Jessica Kingsley Publishers
An Hachette Company

3

Copyright © Joe Brummer 2021
Foreword copyright © Judy Atkinson 2021

A CIP catalogue record for this title is available from the
British Library and the Library of Congress

ISBN 978 1 78775 267 2
eISBN 978 1 78775 268 9

Jessica Kingsley Publishers' policy is to use papers that are natural,
renewable, and recyclable products and made from wood grown in
sustainable forests. The logging and manufacturing processes are expected
to conform to the environmental regulations of the country of origin.

Jessica Kingsley Publishers
Carmelite House
50 Victoria Embankment
London EC4Y 0DZ

www.jkp.com

Printed and bound by CPI Group (UK) Ltd, Croydon, CR0 4YY

This book is dedicated to the memory of two educators who were believers and advocates of trauma-informed restorative practices:

Danielle Fasciocco 1989–2018
and
Raymond Southland 1961–2019

Contents

Section 1: The Foundations, Principles, and a New Understanding of Behavior

Section 2: The Five Skills of Restorative

Section 3: Restorative in Action

Section 4: Implementation

Foreword

Joe Brummer writes: "this book has been a labor of love and healing." Yet, it is clear this "labor of love" is balanced by clear and meaningful intent of purpose, and a sound toolkit for essential social change.

Restorative justice (in schools) is one of the most important initiatives we can endorse at this time. While the book covers *Becoming a Trauma-Informed Restorative School* the skills and approaches are for all situations, relevant to all peoples, everywhere. We all have a responsibility to consider how we can improve the cultures in which we live, and how our behavior reflects and contributes to those cultures. As we become more fully aware of and accept responsibility for our ill health or well-being, the social circumstances and behaviors within which we live, we can see clearly the opportunities offered to us by Joe Brummer to change what needs to be changed. Societies would benefit as a whole.

Perhaps *story* is important here. Eight years ago I was visited by a now close friend, school teacher/psychologist/principal, who had been asked to consider a principal-ship appointment at a school for (Aboriginal) children who had been expelled or suspended from all other schools in the region. They were considered "bad—unteachable—on a fast track to juvenile detention—prison." My friend moved to her new position, five hours drive away. Over the next three months we talked every afternoon, trying to understand the children's behavior. Then a crisis. We located a child psychiatrist and received a diagnosis for one of the children. *Emerging psychosis with some paranoia—he believes the world is unsafe. Suicide ideation. Complex loss and grief. Complex compound post traumatic stress disorder.* This child was not paranoid. His world was unsafe. At three years of age, he had seen his mother killed in a domestic assault, and just before he went into crisis he had seen his aunt, who was his carer, hit and killed by a truck. He had attempted suicide twice, which had triggered our concern. However, his medical records said he was "attention seeking." He was prescribed Ritalin and referred for speech therapy.

After this experience, the principal decided to bring theory into an Indigenous Healing Practice in response to the needs of the children in the school. She organized a skills development workshop over a weekend, grounded in trauma-informed restorative practices while also drawing on the theory and work principles of Dr. Bruce Perry. Sometime later, one Monday morning, those skills became vital.

Behavior on Friday afternoon is chaotic as children anticipate the weekend when drugs hit town. Monday is worse when they return to school. This Monday "Billy" had managed to bring a large carving knife to school, threatening the school community. The school went into lockdown as Billy ran riot around the grounds. The principal walked out into the grounds near him, without looking at him or physically engaging with him, but close enough for him to hear her. "Billy, I always knew you wanted to be a ninja." Billy was in an extreme disassociated state, but her words reached him. He stopped his frenzy for a moment. "Ninjas are really clever. Can you show me how you can throw that knife and make it stand up in the ground?" He hesitated, then focused on throwing the knife, where it stood on an angle in the ground. "Yes," she said, "You are a good Ninja. But you can do better. Try again." By this time Billy was starting to focus on her. He retrieved the knife and threw it again. She was now close enough to engage with him, and again she praised his skills as she turned towards him, suggesting he have another go. He retrieved the knife as she told him he was a very good Ninja and she knew he could make that knife stand up straight in the ground. He was now in eye contact with her, then returned his focus to throwing the knife again. It stood up straight and she gave praise for his Ninja skills, while suggesting he now bring the knife to her, which he did.

I wanted to know where the principal had learnt such skills, to respond to the distressed child in this manner. I have seen many professionals escalate a heightened, dangerous situation. She explained. Be calm in times of crisis. Observe the child (in this case, enough to know he was disassociated, and understand that there was a story behind his behavior). Allow him to connect when he is ready, but keep him engaged. Do not challenge or push—connect but in a non-confrontational way. Build on his interest and strength, she knew he loved Ninja stories. She was already prepared for chaos when she was told a shipment of drugs had come into town on the Friday. She was hence aware that his weekend may have been unsafe, and because she knew the history of the family, she knew his behavior was the language of his weekend trauma—we later found out his mother had been stabbed yet again that weekend. Her objective was to disarm him without force, or harm to his already fragile state.

We learn valuable lessons "on the ground." This book is a good balance of such valuable lessons with sound theory to practice examples.

In Section 1, "The Foundations, Principles, and a New Understanding of Behavior," Joe writes of the need for a new lens in awareness, including understanding the trauma in the lives and behaviors of young people. In asking us to consider the four vital elements—restorative language in community building, repairing relationships, and rebuilding communal attachment—he provides a vital foundation for working with schools for change. However, these are not just skills for schools—they are for whole communities and societies.

It is, however, in Section 2 that possibilities started to unfold for me, in the schools I know in Australia. The Five Skills of Restorative—mindfulness, empathy, honest expression, the art of asking questions, and requests—were all present in the principal's response to Billy's distressed behavior. She taught me, as Joe also points out, restorative is within yourself. It is a way of being. And in that, the responsibility of adults working with children is to nurture discipline—mastery of which, as Joe writes, is cultivated. I am a gardener. During this time of Covid-19 I have turned soil and planted seeds. In the cultivation, the planting, and watering of seeds and seedlings I pondered the outcomes for children in the richness of a restorative cultivation. Can children teach us?

One cold winter's morning, a child came to school with no shoes, a flimsy tee-shirt, and shorts. Freezing. Next day we saw children come to school with warm clothing to gift him. These were extremely poor families and yet the cultivation of mindfulness and empathy in the school provided a rich harvest, allowing us to see loving kindness in action. More particularly in the first full year of the application of a trauma-responsive, restorative practice in this school for "bad" kids, not only did children teach us loving kindness in action, but their literacy and numeracy levels under the Australian National Assessment Program—Literacy and Numeracy (NAPLAN) improved by between 150 percent and 300 percent (School Annual report 2014). The school, guided by the wisdom of an

Aboriginal Elder: "some trees need more water than others," taught us lessons about restorative in action.

The lessons learned in "Restorative in Action" (Section 3) allowed me to reflect on what our school learnt in our work with the children and their families. Joe writes: "restorative is best when we spend about 60 percent building community." The school became a drop-in center for parents, grandparents, and carers of the children. Accidental counseling happened, often. These were adults who had not had good experiences when they had attended school. The parents of the children at this school were only allowed to enter school, at the discretion of a principal, in the 1970s. The cane was used extensively. The Aboriginal students were not allowed to go to the swimming pool on Friday afternoons and had to stay behind and clean the school yards, while the rest of the school spent the afternoon at the swimming pool. Such were the experiences of the parents of the children at our school.

Now in a restorative approach, the school has run community-based workshops and the community is asking for more. In understanding more deeply the needs of the children the door has been opened to work across the community. Joe writes: "30 percent of restorative time is working collaboratively and proactively to address unsolved problems, conflicts, or harm of the children." Confronting the failure of service systems, advocating for the children, challenging the multiple Government and Non-Government Organizations was hard work. But with in-school advocacy for the children's needs, services started to change.

Joe writes: "10 percent of the time was to address more serious interventions." Even when some of what was done felt like failure and a young person went away for a time to juvenile detention, on release they often came back to the school to say hello. This however is where the real work is, and Joe is clear: restorative in action is essential for society as a whole.

While regulations demand respectful behavior by children towards teachers, in the school observations were teachers who did not reciprocate in their attitudes and actions towards the children. Behaviors changed after a workshop was run which outlined possible responses to children with developmental trauma, which could be embedded within curriculum. The response by the children and their families and carers was immediate. In reciprocity, children who felt appreciated and accepted in the school taught teachers to change their attitudes and behaviors.

In the first section of Joe's book, we spend time learning about the "why" of this work. We learn that understanding trauma provides a reason to deepen trauma-responsive skills so that schools can provide safe learning environments, for all our children and young people. The book is clear. We need to change what we are doing if it is not working for our children of the future. In our school when we changed, when we ran trauma-specific training and the school changed, the children changed, families started to change, and the community asked for help to change. More importantly the educational system has started to change, and that, in this instance, is a big story for another time.

The second section of Joe's book introduces skills for action. Use and adaption of such skills can improve our professional practice and our ability to connect with each other and the children who want to learn from us. Our experience, however, is that in applying those skills for action we also change. Healing happens within.

The third section allows us to consider what these ideas look like in practice. Like any practice, it takes time and change is incremental. However, we can already see the change. Example after example is given in the book. Hence the book can become a template for embracing the true meaning of the word "education." From the Greek, to the Latin, to the English: to rear up, to nurture the children, to draw out from them, to lead, to show the way. This is a good time to learn, for when we move into what Joe has called Section 4, "Implementation," we can learn together, through the power of shared stories.

As Joe writes: "Having trauma-informed restorative schools isn't the end of the road. It *is* the road. The end is healthy communities." We need healthy families and communities, everywhere.

Judy Atkinson
Emeritus Professor (Honorary)
Member of the Order of Australia
Founder and Patron of We Al-li

Acknowledgments

There are more people to thank on the journey to writing this book than I could possibly fit on a page. I would like to list a few by name for their direct contributions, encouragement, and support to the journey of healing that ultimately has become this book and the story it tells: Chris Thomas, Tom and Carol Hollenden, Connie and Bill Noll, Carl and Maryjane Brummer, Mario Florez, Sarah Diggs, Amy Miglore, Rick Kelly, Nann Starr, Martha Brown, Dorothy Vaandering, Kathy Evans, Jim and Jean Walker, Jim Collin, Miguel Cardona, Gail DeBlasio, Justin Carbonella, Joanne and Matt Wilcox, Jim Sporleder, Dennis Littky, Kitty Tyrol, Susan Earley, Carolyn Boyes-Watson, Jen Zehler, Melissa Sadin, Suzanne Duran-Crelin, Thea Martin, Pam Guest, Eric Lopez, Leonard Jahad, Lynda Thorton, Barbara Nimmer, Geoff Kenyon, Lee Rush, Tracy Prete, David Howe, and the dozens and dozens of educators who allowed me into their classrooms.

I want to acknowledge Dr. Ross Greene and Annie O'Shaughnessy for the mentoring of the chapters that involved their work. I deeply appreciate the support and time you offered me. Thank you.

Finally, I want to thank Margaret Thorsborne for her guidance in editing this book. The encouragement and belief in this project were the fuel to help me finish it. I also want to thank my husband and love, Rick Cain, for his support and his work on this book. None of this would have been possible without him.

Preface

In the spring of 1990, on a warm evening, I found myself the unfortunate victim of a violent anti-LGBT hate crime. I was badly beaten and left for dead as I had rolled myself into a nearby river to escape those inflicting this harm on me. I would be dead had it not been for some passersby who happened to fish me out because they heard the commotion. To compound the trauma, my sexuality was still closeted. In my attempts to keep that secret guarded and safe, I was almost arrested by the police who were annoyed that I could not keep my story straight. The fears of being outed and of being arrested were more painful than the physical injuries. In the days, weeks, and years it has taken me to heal, it left me curious more than anything.

As fate might have it in May of 2000, I was leaving a popular LGBT nightclub late one night and again became the victim of an anti-LGBT hate crime, this time being body-slammed to the ground as I exited the club, while a group of young men ran down the street yelling slurs about gay people. My friends ran after the group and abandoned that effort when they noticed I remained unconscious on the pavement in the middle of the road. I was left with severe injuries, including a concussion and broken clavicle. My curiosity became stronger to understand why people do what they do, and to comprehend why some people on our planet are willing, if not happy, to inflict suffering on others. These events, along with a childhood filled with emotional and physical abuse, bullying, and the struggle of being gay put me on a journey to learn about peace, justice, and healing. This book is a part of that ongoing journey into healing.

I wrote this book for educators and other adults who come into contact with children and youth with the hope I could change the lens through which you see their struggles. Years of trying to figure out violence and nonviolence have led me to conclude many of the social ills I see around me stem from the impacts of trauma including homophobia, racism, classism, and sexism. Our prisons are filled with traumatized people and our response furthers that trauma. Our addiction clinics are also filled with traumatized people. As you continue to read, you will learn about the correlation between negative health, social challenges, and trauma. I deeply believe that if we can limit the experiences of toxic stress in our children's lives, we won't raise children who inflict violence on others or themselves. This is no small task and yet it is worth doing.

My goal with this book is to introduce you to the powerful ideas that my journey has introduced to me. These are ideas that I believe could make schools and communities stronger and less violent. Restorative Justice, Nonviolent Communication™, and mindfulness have changed my life and the way I see the events I have survived. I hope that sharing these philosophies, skills, and practices will change you.

Introduction

On a spring day, just days before the last day of school, I stopped by one of the schools where I was working as a consultant. I was asked if I would bring a cup of coffee to a substitute teacher who had a migraine and needed some caffeine relief. I was happy to be the bringer of such relief to someone in pain. When I got into the class, the sub was lecturing a room full of very unhappy fourth-grade students about how she "had it up to here with this behavior." If it continued, she said with an irritated face, she "would be forced to start taking things away." I thought to myself for a moment that one of the mistakes teachers can make with students is being hyper-focused on controlling behavior and getting compliance. When trying to get our way with others, we do it at the expense of long-term influence over their future choices. We do it at the expense of the relationship.

On another occasion, I was visiting friends for a summer holiday and listening to a woman who was there with her best friend's daughter. I watched and listened to their various interactions and communication, perhaps being a little sensitive because it was during a time when I was reading several books on child development, communication, and discipline. At one point, the child wanted to go home to her mom, which wasn't possible, so when told she couldn't go home yet, the girl whined as children may do when distressed. In reply, the woman said, "I am the adult here and you are the child." That line has always burned me a little and, for some reason, it punched me in the stomach that day. Translating that to a child's ears with a child's developmental brain stage, I imagined that what the young girl heard was "I matter, and you don't." I was deeply saddened by the message sent to this child.

Relationships matter in the classroom, in our families, and in our community organizations where children and youth will interact with adults. I am not always fond of the way I see some children and youth being treated by adults. As if it is somehow an adult's job to "make children and adolescents behave," rather than teach them the skills it takes to be a contributing member of the community. I believe how we talk to children (and each other) matters!

In this book, I explain the concepts of Nonviolent Communication, Restorative Justice, mindfulness, and Collaborative and Proactive Solutions™ (CPS) (Figure I.1). I want to do my best to frame each of these in the light of a trauma-informed approach. Each of these concepts and philosophies is extremely powerful on its own, and I believe the strengths and weaknesses of each balance the other in the school, work, and community setting. I also want each of these approaches to be seen through the lens of equity and racial justice.

Figure I.1: An integrated implementation

This book is an attempt to synthesize the implementation of these theories and models so there is less burnout for educators, and we capitalize on the overlaps in principles and foundations. Often when implemented, each is done in isolation, and I would like to see all these approaches implemented as one orchestrated initiative. I believe school staff becomes incredibly stressed when we try to implement too many initiatives at once; yet, if we combine the implementation, we can make it more doable. When we implement these concepts in a coordinated way, we can manage the contradictions while still holding fidelity to individual models. For example, a singing bowl or a chime in the mindfulness community would only be used to signal the start and end of meditation. We would not use it to get attention in a classroom as that may confuse students about the meaning of the chime. In other classroom models, chimes are used to gain attention from students.

In this book, I am going to use the term *restorative* to refer to all the philosophies and practices that encompass this paradigm shift in human thinking about the ideas of rightness and wrongness. This thinking is a move away from the idea that any of us know what is right, wrong, good, or bad, because those terms are too over-simplified to explain the true nature of what and why we do what we do. The Sufi poet Rumi said it well: "Somewhere out there beyond the ideas of rightdoing and wrongdoing, there is a field. I will meet you there."

From doing work with parents, educators, and even supervisors in the workplace, it quickly became clear to me that many people still see discipline as something you do *to* people rather than something that is cultivated. This distinction is important for changing the relationships we have with students, employees, and even our own children. If we want to nurture discipline in others, we need to take a hard look at our framework, including the words we use and the actions we take in response. Restorative is not something you *do*; it is something you *are* within yourself. It is a way of being.

We throw the words discipline, punishment, consequences, and accountability around as if they are interchangeable. Take a moment to reflect on those words. What do they mean to you? How are they different? They are not interchangeable, because each of these words has very different meanings and, even more so, they have very different outcomes. This is a huge problem when trying to move to a restorative approach to development. We use words like consequences or discipline when we mean punishment, simply because it makes it sound better. It isn't better. This goes beyond simple semantics. It's about really being honest about our intentions with both ourselves and others. Let's begin by rethinking the language we use and choose words that accurately describe what we are doing and feeling.

Most dictionaries and even some experts will tell you that discipline is a verb as well as a noun. Personally, I don't like using discipline as a verb. For me, discipline isn't something you do; it's something you nurture. I see discipline as the internalized motivation to practice self-regulation, whereas punishment is external control; discipline is the internal willingness to sit and practice the piano because practice improves a skill; it is a need for mastery. Punishment causes a person to practice the piano in fear of what we will do to them if they don't. This is what psychologist William Glasser (1998), in his book *Choice Theory: A New Psychology of Personal Freedom*, called external control psychology. Discipline involves the person choosing to act based on internal reasoning versus external manipulation.

One of the goals of punishment is usually to demand compliance with rules through suffering. Such tactics are nothing short of manipulation. External reasoning almost always involves the fear of punishment or the promise of rewards. Compliance gets you a student or employee who is doing what you want in fear of punishment or for the promise of a reward. We don't want compliance unless there is a concern for safety. What happens when the external control is taken away? There is no reason to be compliant. It gets you what Marshall Rosenberg (2004) called "nice polite dead people" (p.14). You will hear me say again and again in this book that I believe we have enough suffering in the world and don't need to add more of it to our children's lives.

What we want is engagement. We want our children and youth or those we supervise to see the reason behind behaving a certain way and developing a sense of discipline around it. If a teacher is using external control to get compliance, it is almost guaranteed that class will be a train-wreck when they have a substitute teacher who can't get the same compliance. Children and youth don't see the benefit to themselves other than not getting punished. A further illustration of this comes from Alfie Kohn (2006) in his book *Unconditional Parenting: Moving from Rewards and Punishments to Love and Reason* in which he references the research of others who found that "parents who punish[ed] rule-breaking behavior in their children at home often had children who demonstrated higher levels of rule-breaking when away from home" (location 1080). It's the same idea: If you take away the threat, you take away the reason to be compliant.

Let's take a moment to acknowledge that too often the word consequence is a secret code for punishment. Adults often try to use the term consequences for things that are punishments. A few years ago, I was doing some work with interns and staff at a youth organization in New Haven, Connecticut. The interns were all teenagers who would be working with younger children to teach them about being stewards of the environment and leadership. When one of the adult staff expressed some confusion about the differences between punishment and consequences, a youth intern named Corey eloquently and with much excitement said, "Oh, I got this one: You can't make up consequences. You need to make up punishments." I thought this was a brilliant understanding, and no surprise it came from a teenage member of the organization. The consequences are simple. You go out in the rain, you get wet. You spill milk, it makes a mess. When you speak unkindly of others, you won't have many friends. Consequences are about a cause and effect, and they exist naturally in the world. Our goal with restorative is always to help people see the consequences of their actions. In other words, we are talking about impact. This will help them develop internal reasoning for their future behaviors. This is the difference between getting control over students versus influencing their future choices.

A note does need to be made here about culture and punishment. Punishment, in many cultures around the world, was not a part of parenting or culture until the arrival of colonialism. One aspect of colonialism is the belief that the white, Christian, European way of doing things is the right way of doing things. This means stripping people of many cultures of their Indigenous parenting styles. In the USA, the system of racism forced Black parents to abandon traditional African ways of raising children and to adopt ways that protected children from white slave owners, angry mobs, and the police. It became a survival issue for parents to teach their children that they need compliance the first time something is asked for and this sadly became a further source of trauma for Black families.

It is all about influence! To cultivate a sense of internal discipline, we need to use influence developed through relationships. Influence is about input and guidance over future choices of behavior. Punishment hinders this process because it damages the relationship, causes resentment, and, therefore, decreases the influence we have over future choices. This is the recognition that we can't make people do stuff! We only have the power to influence their future choices (Glasser 1998). All our behaviors are a choice; hence, the only way to build influence is to build a relationship. This is hard when you have 30 little faces smiling at you in the classroom or you're staring into the eyes of your own child when they have just been suspended for fighting or have torn up the living room.

To build influence, it is necessary to check our own emotions (i.e., being mindful) and make sure we aren't reacting from anger or frustration. Then connect with the behavior instead of judging it as *right* or *wrong* or *good* or *bad*. Connect with what the other person is thinking and feeling at the time they chose to act. Talk about the impact of the actions and then talk about new behaviors. Everyone can benefit from seeing this as a problem to solve, not a behavior to control. The next step will always be to think about what outcomes are wanted and what will make those happen in the best interest of the child. This changes the paradigm from expressing our anger through punishment to planning out the building of skills to behave better. Influence is built over time, whereas compliance is gained in the moment by anyone using power-over strategies. Influence is built on trust and relationship. All humans have the desire to be in a good relationship with others (Boyes-Watson and Pranis 2015). When you work off this premise, we are far more likely to see others' behavior as attempts to meet needs, rather than purposeful actions meant to irritate or annoy.

Countless teachers have come and gone who are convinced student behavior is designed solely to push their buttons or irritate them. That type of conventional wisdom says that students are out to either get something or avoid something. Such a view of behavior leaves little chance of seeing what is actually behind the behavior. In some cases, student behavior could be influenced by unprocessed feelings, trauma, boredom, or, more likely, a lack of skills. You don't know until you build a connection and relationship. I was working with 6th-grade teachers in a kindergarten through to 8th-grade school in New Haven, Connecticut. They described to me a student who was misbehaving in the class and constantly disturbing other students. Other students were happy when this student stayed home. They claimed to have tried everything to manage his behavior. I inquired as to how much one-on-one time they had with this student. Immediately, they replied, "We don't have time for that." Surely, they could see how much time they already invested trying to get compliance, with no change, from a child they had little relationship with in the first place. Why would he want to change his behavior for people with whom he doesn't have a sense of connection or trust? They had not built their influence with him. All they could hope for was that external bribes or threats were working—which they were not.

In a truly restorative classroom, influence is all around. Teachers are not the only influence to behave in ways that benefit the group. In a restorative classroom, circles and restorative dialogue are used to build enough trust between students so that they influence each other's behavior in positive ways. That only happens when time is invested in students being in a relationship with each other! This is also true of the workplace as trauma-informed schools need to be trauma-informed workplaces. Supervisors have a much better chance of getting great work from an employee with whom they have connection and influence than an employee who doesn't have a sense of belonging to the team.

SECTION SUMMARIES

This book lays out the practices that need to change and the skills needed for educators to be able to get the most from these practices. With all that said, none of these will help anyone if the practices and skills are not grounded in solid change as to how we view children's and adolescents' behaviors.

Section 1: (Chapters 1–3) The Foundations, Principles, and a New Understanding of Behavior

Section 1 is meant to change the lens through which we see relationships and behavior. It helps to map out the roots of a child's behavior and how it is impacted by trauma, community, relationships, and education. Once we change the lens, we begin to change from seeing children and youth *in-trouble* to seeing them *in-struggle*.

Section 2: (Chapters 4–9) The Five Skills of Restorative

These chapters help us build the skill sets we need to live out the principles in Section 1. Being *motivated* to do things differently also requires the *ability* to do things differently, from being present to listening and talking in new ways to learning how to ask deeper questions. This section will offer you the skills that allow you to live out this change.

Section 3: (Chapters 10–15) Restorative in Action

This section offers some introductions to various practices we can use to build a positive school community. While it is in no way meant to have you master any of these practices, it will help you to begin your journey into this work and transform your school.

Section 4: (Chapter 16) Implementation

This chapter lays out considerations and planning to begin implementing trauma-informed restorative practices. From the district level to the classroom, it explores what change management issues to address. It also looks at ways to keep up momentum in the face of obstacles, and celebrate our successes to help build a better school climate.

All pages marked with a ✷ can be downloaded at www.jkp.com/catalogue/book/9781787752672 or from www.joebrummer.com for your personal use.

THE FOUNDATIONS, PRINCIPLES, AND A NEW UNDERSTANDING OF BEHAVIOR

CHAPTER 1

A New Lens on Behavior

INTRODUCTION

It can be challenging for some people to understand that Restorative Justice is about *how living justly* creates community. The concept of being restorative places the community at the center of well-being, something Indigenous people have known for centuries. Rather than focusing on economic growth or shareholder gains, restorative bases everything we do on how well it serves the community. Rather than creating systems that pit people against each other in competition or how to outdo others, we seek collaboration and realize that when we are uplifting others, we are also uplifting ourselves. Restorative principles and practices are more than responding to harm through criminal courts, suspensions, punishments, creating replacements for discipline systems, or new ways of handling wrongdoing. They are about prevention. This is about addressing and dismantling systems that create harm in the first place, including systems that leave some people with less power than others. Fania Davis (2019), founder of Restorative Justice for Oakland Youth, supports this argument in her book *The Little Book of Race and Restorative Justice* (p.21):

> Contemporary Restorative Justice arises alongside the historical backdrop of heightened international awareness that indigenous knowledges, grounded in an ecological ethos of interrelatedness and collaboration, have much to offer today's fractured world. The corollary is the growing recognition that for more than five hundred years, Western knowledge systems, based on an ethos of separateness, competition, and subordination, have contributed to pervasive crises that today imperil our future. The scale of devastation is unprecedented—whether of our bodies, families, and communities, or plants, animals, waters and earth. The unfathomable magnitude of destruction has fueled a quest

for alternative worldviews that bring healing to our world. It is in this historical context that we witness the rapid global rise and spread of Restorative Justice.

In this chapter, we gain a deeper understanding of how *to be* restorative by exploring a different way of seeing relationships and community and examining the ways in which we build and hold those relationships together even when harm has been introduced. We address the widespread use of punishments and rewards as consequences to behavior and examine why simply addressing motivation does not produce change. We will gain an understanding that all human behavior is grounded in trying to meet basic universal human needs and is part of the foundation of how we interact and connect with others when trying to get those needs met. As such, we begin to develop a new lens through which we see relationships and connection as opportunities and solutions to challenging behaviors.

PUNISHMENT AS VIOLENCE

The actor is, in their own mind, punishing the receiver because they believe it is deserved because those are the "bad" people. Much violence, if not all violence, is retaliation not to a person's actions but the actor's perceptions. The main goal of punishment is to make the wrongdoer suffer. We try to make the suffering fit the crime, reminiscent of an eye for an eye, tit-for-tat, or other forms of retribution. How is that *not* violence when our goal is to make others suffer? While viewing punishment as violence may seem like an extreme idea for some, its use seems to continue as a means of controlling others, and the negative outcomes are many. What is important to know about most children and adolescents is that just the threat of punishment is enough to regulate their behavior because they do have the skills to respond to these threats. While that seems positive, it sadly teaches students that using threats is a valid way of doing things. It also means they are driven by the fear of what we will do to them.

Children are not born with executive functioning skills—these are developmental. If children and adolescents are not provided with what they need from positive and supportive adult relationships and an environment free of toxic stress (e.g., one that is safe and free of violence and neglect, with opportunities for creativity and exploration), their experiences can be delayed or impaired (Harvard University n.d.), resulting in what Greene (2008) refers to as lagging skills. Cognitive flexibility or being flexible in our thinking is an example of an executive functioning skill. Cognitive flexibility, when lagging, shows up in a child who screams when you change the rules of a game and says, "That's not how you play" or with a child who just can't stop one task to move to another because "I'm not done." Another example would be with problem-solving and having the capacity to set one's emotions to one side for a moment in order to examine other available options and possibly choose one that best solves the problem at hand.

Punishments do not teach the lagging thinking skills which created the problem that caused the behavior that caused the need for the punishment in the first place (Greene 2008). For those who are lacking the skills for self-regulation, especially if they have trauma in their background, the threat of punishment is more likely to deregulate their nervous system, cause reactance, and escalate it to possibly unmanageable or even dangerous levels. This is because they lack the skills to respond or they have developed survival strategies meant to keep them in control and safe, and this may look like defiance to adults. When we add stress to already stressed-out children and youth, this can lead to more behavioral issues, not fewer (Markham 2019). Moreover, punishment rarely results in positive changes in behavior and may result in subversive or in temporary suppression of behavior; at best, it produces compliance (Crawford, Bodine and Hoglund 1993). Teaching children what you don't expect of them fails to teach what you do expect.

Punishments can be demoralizing—that is, children and adolescents feel shame about who they are, rather than understanding the consequences of what they did. Punishment reinforces a failure identity and, the more you use it, the more children own the identity as someone who needs it. It creates an external locus of control. As such, children begin to see the adult or parent as the authority figure and as responsible for making them behave, rather than taking responsibility for their behavior as their own choice (Markham 2019). It also sends the message that when you aren't doing your best, people will hurt you more or send you away. Punishment promotes a loss of confidence and motivation, and children who are punished sometimes feel they can't do anything right and then stop trying.

Punishment leads children to focus on their suffering from the punishment, rather than on the harm they may have caused to others.

Punishment also tends to focus on the child responsible for creating harm. It often fails to address those impacted. When we pull a student out of class for disruptions, we often forget the other students who were harmed by this action (Zehr 2015). Adults tend to believe they teach children to be responsible for their behavior by imposing the punishment when, in reality, being responsible for your behavior means making things right, rather than serving a punishment. In children and adolescents, punishment encourages a lack of responsibility and accountability. It teaches lying, sneaking, blaming, and how to avoid getting caught. Punishment models bullying by teaching that threats, intimidation, purposeful ignoring, taking valued items or privileges away, and exclusion are acceptable ways of getting what you want (Kohn 2016). Again, punishments sadly teach children and adolescents that using threats is a valid way of doing things.

The American Academy of Pediatrics published a policy paper titled "Effective discipline to raise healthy children" (Sege and Siegel 2018), which updated the organization's position and urged parents and caregivers to end the use of corporal punishments. The Academy explained that, especially in younger children, spanking, hitting, shaking, and other forms of physical pain can leave serious and long-lasting physical and psychological damage. Children and youth raised in homes using physical punishment have higher chances of substance abuse, interacting with law enforcement, and dropping out of school. Studies also show that physical punishment leads to changes in the brain and developmental delays. You don't even have to hit teenagers to harm them. Wang and Kenny (2014) showed that using harsh verbal punishments (defined as shouting, cursing, or using insults) may be just as detrimental to the long-term well-being of adolescents as hitting them. Rather than curbing problematic behavior, it appears that yelling and dishing our verbal punishment may increase it. When we were younger many of us saw our friends shrink when their parents or teachers yelled at them, belittled them, called them names like stupid, disrespectful, or brat, or shamed them with statements like "You should know better."

If people looked at the goals and outcomes they hope to achieve from any intervention, either restorative or punitive, and then evaluated whether those goals were met, they would stop using punishment. In the school environment, the general goals of intervening tend to focus on changing the behavior, keeping the school safe, maintaining community and relationship, cultivating internal discipline, and changing or teaching a lesson about that behavior. Since suspension is a common disciplinary action in schools, its purpose may be worth examining. Let's say a student was in a fight at school and the administration decided to employ the suspension strategy.

- Does suspension change the behavior? Not likely. The use of physical violence is not likely to be affected by sending the student home for ten days, because suspension does not teach any new skills about managing the frustration or anger that caused the student to be violent.

- Does sending the student home keep the school safe? Maybe on a temporary level, but it will not have changed the school safety level when the student returns, because no new skills were gained from the suspension and we still have unsolved problems challenging that student.

- Does sending the student home maintain community and relationship? Unlikely, because sending the student home also does not change the fact that violence was introduced into the school community and is now part of the narrative for other students.

- Does sending the student home stimulate internal discipline? This is also unlikely as the student most likely sees the suspension as something done *to* him or her and, therefore, puts the responsibility for the harm on others. The effect is intensified if the student was sent home on suspension in less than ideal circumstances, like not having access to food, electricity, or supervision.

- Does it teach the student a lesson about fighting? It is doubtful if the student is unable to make the connection between fighting and the punishment. That is a high expectation from a child or adolescent when, developmentally, they may not have the ability to establish a connection between punishment and the impact of violence on oneself and others.

- That begs the final question: Did sending this student home for a ten-day suspension achieve any of the goals we had to intervening?

REWARDS

According to Deci and Flaste (1995), rewards are both autonomous (intrinsic) and controlled (external). When a reward is autonomous, one is acting in accord with one's own free will—that is, the interest is authentic, the individual is willing, engaged with a sense of interest, and committed to meeting their own needs and those of others. When external, an individual is not acting in harmony of meeting the needs of the self and others. An individual may perform the behavior without a sense of personal engagement, feel pressured, controlled, and alienated. Deci and Flaste explain that when reacting to controlled behavior, one is either being compliant (i.e., doing what one is told) or defiant (i.e., doing the opposite of what is expected). On the other hand, a person can act autonomously yet do so with the sense of obligation; that is, they perform a behavior as expected just because it is expected.

There are several reasons why students can benefit from stopping reliance on rewards or token economy systems. Rewards become an external motivator that is great for simple tasks yet leads to problems when it comes to teaching higher-order thinking skills (Pink 2009). Rewards also encourage behaviors we may not want. In one school district where I consulted, the assistant superintendent said he once caught a group of middle schoolers making photocopies of Positive Behavior Interventions and Supports coupons to sell to fellow students. Offering rewards can also decrease interest in the learning activity; if instead the learning is reward-driven and the rewards stop, this can increase the likelihood of the behavior stopping (Deci and Flaste 1995; Kohn 1993). Kohn also states that rewards may be dehumanizing because they are a way to control people, and Mulvahill (2018) indicates that rewards can affect a student's self-esteem if their self-validation is based on external factors. Rewards can also encourage cheating and unethical behavior (Pink 2009).

Essentially, everything anyone does is done with an intrinsic motivation to satisfy one or more needs (Glasser 1998). When you add extrinsic factors like punishments, the reward may switch to survival or not being punished. Rewards are consequences and are best avoided if students are to take responsibility for their own behavior and the teacher wants to promote the internalization of positive values and not obedience (Kohn 1994).

IN THE SERVICE OF MEETING NEEDS

All human behavior is in the service of meeting basic universal human needs. This isn't a new concept, as Abraham Maslow proposed the idea of human motivation being based on a hierarchy of needs in an article titled "A theory of human motivation" (Maslow 1943). Glasser (1998) in his work on Choice Theory proposed all behavior is in the service of one of five main needs: survival, fun, love, power, and freedom (see Table 1.1).

Table 1.1: Basic universal human needs

Survival	Fun	Love and belonging	Freedom	Power
Food	Play	Connection	Autonomy	Influence
Health	Entertainment	Trust/Honesty	Independence	Achievement
Shelter	Excitement	Empathy	Individuality	Recognition
Warmth	Laughter	Appreciation	Self-empowerment	Competence
Water	Passion	Community	Solitude	Efficiency
Safety	Enjoyment	Family	Choice	Value
Security	Learning	Friendship		
Protection	Growth	Respect		
Rest	Mastery	Affection		
Air	Teaching	Purpose		
		Meaning		

Source: Adapted from Glasser (1998)

Peace activist and clinical psychologist Marshall Rosenberg (2003b, 2015) made meeting needs a center focus of his concept of Nonviolent Communication. Even the motivation guru Tony Robbins (2006) states that needs are the focus of motivation in his TED Talk, *Why We Do What We Do*. Howard Zehr (2015), sometimes referred to as the grandfather of the modern Restorative Justice movement, supports this needs theory in his book *Changing Lenses: Restorative Justice for Our Time* (p.192):

> Justice that aims to fill and overflow must begin by identifying and seeking to meet human needs. With crime, the starting point must be the needs of those violated. When a crime occurs (regardless of whether an "offender" is identified), the first questions ought to be, "Who has been harmed?"; "How have they been harmed?"; and "What are their needs?" Such an approach would, of course, be far from that of retributive justice, which first asks, "Who did it?" and "What should be done to them?"—and then rarely moves beyond that point.

Words are what adults use to label their feelings and needs and to name their experience. Babies do not yet have the words to name their experience, so when they cry or laugh, they are using that behavior to share that a need is either met or not met. As children grow and develop through adolescence, they learn to match what they are feeling with words that name to themselves and to others whether needs are met or unmet. With this understanding, it is important to realize that even adults will have difficulty naming their experience using the correct words, so why fault children and youth when we know that this understanding is developmental through adulthood?

When we can see people's behavior as an attempt to meet their needs, we can rethink our assumptions about manipulation, coercion, attention-seeking, and so on, and this will help us to avoid the trap of blame and judgment. This awakening draws us to want to connect at the needs level to solve our conflicts. This also requires us to acknowledge no one's needs trump another's needs. Our needs are equal and in no way in competition with each other. Our strategies on the other hand are often at odds, in competition, or confusing—and that is where conflict lives.

We want to change from moral to value judgments. Restorative asks us to see others' actions outside of the blame box of judging them as right, wrong, good, or bad. Rather than seeing the rightness or wrongness, we want an evaluation if they met or didn't meet our universal basic human needs (see Table 1.2). This may seem like such a small and even insignificant change in thinking and yet it can be transformative. It is helpful to change our thinking from *what* a person did to *how* we think people are. This moves our thinking away from judging others to instead describing our human experiences.

Table 1.2: Needs thinking

Old thinking	Becomes
"Stealing is wrong."	"Stealing doesn't meet my needs for community and safety."
"You're really disrespectful."	"Your actions don't meet my need for respect."
"Can't you see how selfish you are?"	"I really value consideration."

The request for compliance isn't always horrible and, in some cases, demanding compliance is necessary to meet needs for order, safety, and well-being. Yet, sometimes teachers think, "I have to do what I need to do." Just know that demands come at a price. Demanding compliance from a student with challenging behavior could escalate a situation to unsafe levels. It is helpful to first ask yourself, "What is more important in the moment: Getting my way or de-escalating this student back to a regulated state?" You cannot reason and connect with a student who is in any form of fight, flight, or freeze—the body's automatic response to protect us from a perceived threat or danger (there is more about this in Chapter 2). During stress, the frontal cortex functions are impaired. Trying to reason with a person who is hysterical is not likely to calm them down. In fact, telling a person to calm down is likely to be the last thing that will calm them down!

THE RELATIONSHIP MATRIX

To make all this thinking work, we must begin with a goal of connection and relationship. Trust requires a child who values our relationship and opinions, and not a child who resents us. Each time we try to impose our adult will or try to gain compliance through punishment, it is done at the expense of relationship and influence. Adults may get their way in the short term (compliance) while losing ground in the long term (influence).

The Relationship Matrix (see Figure 1.1) displays four different types of relationship that can exist between adults and younger people. Added was information about Collaborative and Proactive Solutions (CPS) (Greene 2008). Each block represents a type of relationship and provides information about how we view and work with others, such as expectations, the amount of support provided, relational power, and connection.

When we see students as objects to manage, we are likely to see them as people we are in relation *to* and therefore have high expectations and provide little support. These types of relationship may place the student's brain into a state of fight-flight-freeze and leave them triggered and anxious. When we power-over students with little support, they will feel like things are being done *to* them and they are likely to comply for a while until the resentment builds, at which point they will just rebel. This is the teacher who demands that a child just puts their headphones away or they will get sent to the office.

When we have low expectations and provide little support to students, we view them *not* as people but as objects to ignore. It basically amounts to a neglectful relationship. On the other hand, when we choose compliance as the goal, we end up with students who see an adult as an authoritarian boss. You don't want to be authoritarian or power-over. I would argue that such a strategy is likely to get you compliance from your students, and they don't learn what we want to teach them.

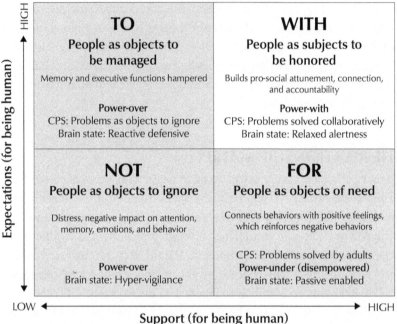

Figure 1.1: *The Relationship Matrix*

We don't want to be stuck in the *for* or permissive box either. When we view others as objects of need where our relationship is *for* them, we take away their power to do things for themselves (low expectations) and provide too much support, which can be very disempowering. Permissive parents are the ones who are too high on the support and not enough on the boundary setting. These are parents who give their child the answer, solve their issues, and fix everything they break, such as when parents leave their jobs at lunchtime to bring forgotten items to their children at school, rather than allow their child to experience the consequences of their actions. It doesn't work because it fails to teach the executive functioning skills children and adolescents need and also fails to teach accountability while disallowing the children to become empowered to take charge of their own lives. Lastly, when you have low boundaries and low support, children and adolescents are in control and they don't have the life skills for that. It is simply neglect. We want them to feel like this is a partnership between parent or teacher and child in growing the child's life skills.

When we see ourselves in relationship *with* students, we view them with high expectations and support. We allow them to be empowered while not losing any of our own power. This power-with model teaches children and adolescents to problem solve, critically think, make choices, and do it *with* us for both clear expectations and support. Set a tone of connection over compliance. Set the tone early that you are there to support them no matter what happens. Failure, trouble, drugs—you are the adult who is there to support them when they mess up and you will help them clean up the mess. They are still accountable for cleaning up the mess they made by repairing the harm. Children and youth need to learn early on that even when you are disappointed in them, you are there to provide support in being the best they can be. You won't send them away as often happens. Restorative in schools suggests we use power structures to work *with* children and adolescents.

CONVENTIONAL VERSUS RESTORATIVE THINKING

To start seeing challenging behaviors as opportunities to teach skills, problem solve, and create relationships, we need a new paradigm. This new approach to seeing behavior as an attempt to meet needs and sometimes having a lack of skills to do so is vital to our implementation of whole-school trauma-informed restorative. This is much different than the conventional thinking we hold now that states children misbehave because they aren't trying hard enough or that they lack motivation. As shown in Table 1.3, it is a move away from thinking our children misbehave to get stuff or avoid responsibility (Greene 2014a, 2014b; Rosenberg 2003b, 2015; Zehr 2015). The philosophy, as Greene (2014b) states often, is "Kids do well if they can" (p.10).

Table 1.3: Conventional versus restorative thinking

Conventional thinking	Restorative thinking
Focus on the rules broken	Focus on the people harmed
Accountability equals punishment	Accountability means addressing the harm

cont.

Conventional thinking	Restorative thinking
Focus on past	Focus on future
Focus on offender	Focus on community
Offender defined by their crime	Offender seen holistically
Focus on crisis management	Focus on crisis prevention
"What's wrong with you?"	"What happened to you?"
Justice focuses on establishment of guilt/innocence	Justice focuses on needs and responsibilities of all involved
All behavior is motivated by external punishments and rewards	All behavior is motivated by basic universal human needs
Challenging behavior is used to get things (e.g., attention) or to escape and avoid things (e.g., work, responsibility)	Behind challenging behavior is a problem to be solved and skills to be learned
Attention seeking	Connection seeking
Behavior is a matter of the child's will	Behavior is a matter of a child's skills
Focused on what people are	Focused on how people are
Outside interventions (court, police)	Community interventions (people most affected by harm)
Focus on control/compliance	Focus on connection/influence/skills
Focus on behavior	Focus on problem-solving
Power-over/under	Power-with
Based on moral judgments	Based on values judgments
Extrinsic motivation	Intrinsic motivation

If we begin to see behaviors as problems to solve rather than something to control or get compliance, we have a better chance to cultivate discipline in students through compassion, not control. The more you are trying to control the person or make another person do something, the more you risk escalation. Imagine trying to take a student's cell phone away the day after they changed foster homes and lost all their other belongings. Perhaps they are accustomed to protecting their things from others. The more the teacher demands to get the phone, the more it is likely to escalate the student's internal defense mechanisms. Placing demands on skills a student does not have or presenting to the student in a way that triggers the threat response is likely to escalate the situation. Pushing any child or adolescent with low frustration tolerance or lagging problem-solving skills to be frustrated with an adult is not only illogical, it could be potentially dangerous to both the adult and child. Unknowingly, teachers walk themselves into dangerous situations when they try to demand compliance from students who have lagging skills around frustration tolerance, cognitive flexibility (adaptability), and problem-solving. In other words, demanding mental flexibility from a younger person who doesn't have it, all the while modeling inflexibility, is not likely to teach the other individual anything about behaving better and will almost guarantee that the individual will explode.

In Chapter 2 we will focus on examining what trauma is, how it impacts the development of a growing brain, and how it shows itself as behavioral challenges in the classroom. We will also examine strategies to reshape our school and classroom environment based on a culture of empathy.

Trauma and the Art of Connection

Understanding the fundamental human need for connection is an essential part of this chapter. We are beings of connection and this is what makes life worth living. Brené Brown (2012), in *Daring Greatly: How the Courage to Be Vulnerable Transforms the Way We Live, Love, Parent, and Lead*, states: "Connection is why we're here. We are hardwired to connect with others, it's what gives purpose and meaning to our lives, and without it there is suffering" (p.7).

A concept of quality of life is belonging, which is the fit between individuals and their environment. Strong relationships, built on trust and respect, become the building blocks of community. Martha Brown (2018) emphasizes in her book, *Creating Restorative Schools: Setting Schools Up to Succeed* (p.9):

> Relational ecology focuses on relationships, which is the absolute foundation of restorative practices. And it says the relationships in a school form a living system, like an ecology in nature. When we nurture our relationships in a school, we are feeding and nurturing the school's ecology, which, as in nature, values and sustains every person and relationship within it.

Understanding how connections work is also important, as argued by Siegel and Payne-Bryson (2014) in their book, *No-Drama Discipline: The Whole-Brain Way to Calm the Chaos and Nurture Your Child's Developing Mind* (p.xxii):

> Connection means that we give our kids our attention, that we respect them enough to listen to them, that we value their contribution to

problem-solving, and that we communicate to them that we're on their side—whether we like the way they're acting or not.

Knowing what trauma is and how it impacts the development of a growing brain is important and, in this chapter, we will learn that many human beings experience some form of trauma in their lives. So, if you are wondering if there is a relationship between trauma and human connection, the answer is yes. We simply don't know who, in our daily travels, is carrying what burden, so just assume everyone is carrying a burden you know nothing about. Understanding trauma helps us to have a better understanding of what it means to be connected. It also helps us to understand behavior outcomes. Because a truly trauma-informed, restorative school is based on relationships and community, we also examine how to reshape our school and classroom environment based on a culture of empathy and connection and explore specific strategies that can be used to create better connections with members of our school community.

EMPATHY

Empathy is one of the key ingredients in creating a connection and is often explained as having three main parts (Goleman 2007). Cognitive empathy is explained as the theory of mind. This is our ability to understand the perspective of another person. It's a form of intuitive mind reading, so to speak. Affective empathy is our ability to read another's emotions. It is the ability to *feel-with* as opposed to *feel-for*. Empathic concern, sometimes referred to as compassionate empathy, is our ability to act on the experience. When we can understand and empathize with each other in the present moment, it is a positive connection and a form of bonding. It doesn't mean we like or dislike the person with whom we are connecting. It doesn't mean we agree with all they believe, or what they've done. It means each of us feels seen, heard, and valued by the other at that moment without judgment. A truly positive connection cannot be achieved without empathy.

Have you ever noticed when you see someone experience pain, it is almost as if you are experiencing that pain too? We often express a reaction to other people's experiences even though it isn't happening to us. In 1992, researchers in Parma, Italy, discovered mirror neurons (De Waal 2009). A group of researchers were doing single-cell testing on motor neurons on a macaque monkey's brain. The meters and machines would ding and ring each time the monkey ate a raisin. Surprisingly, the lights and sounds also went off when one of the researchers came in and grabbed a raisin while the monkey simply watched. The question became "Why is a motor neuron lighting up when the monkey isn't moving, and the researcher is?" The proposed theory was that the neurons would fire off in the same way whether the monkey was doing something or watching someone do something. In other words, there was no difference between seeing and doing. Mirror neurons can also be explained easily by watching someone's face as they observe videos and television programs that show people experiencing mishaps. Shows like *America's Funniest Home Videos* were popular in the 1990s and continued with popular websites such as YouTube. We see someone fall or get hit on the head with a ball and we flinch as if it's happening to us.

> I have played a video clip for my training participants when explaining empathy. In the video, actor Sean Connery, in his role as James Bond in the blockbuster movie *Dr. No*, is lying in bed. We slowly see something crawling its way up his body under the sheets, made even more terrifying with the dark, scary music playing. As it is revealed to us to be a tarantula, I watch the participants in my training squirming and flinching, with some even covering their eyes. As the music in the film gets louder and more intense, the spider slowly crosses Bond's shoulder and moves to the pillow. The second that happens, there is always a collective sigh in the room. Next, Bond jumps up and starts pounding the spider with a shoe—funnily enough, no place near where the spider was last seen. The audience smiles and celebrates the removal of a threat that did not actually threaten them. Why do people react like this? What is it that causes them to flinch as if the spider was on them? Empathy and mirror neurons would be my answer.

To empathize and create a connection with our students, we also need to stay focused on being nonjudgmental, as judgment tends to prevent us from creating an empathic connection. Understanding the developmental stage of a child before we pass any judgment about their actions will be useful for creating trust. When their behavior doesn't meet adult expectations, it may well be that developmentally they are not ready for the demand. This will help us find the best approach when trying to reach out to them for connection. It takes ongoing practice for us to stay in a place of putting our opinions, theories, and sometimes a diagnosis of people to the side and to be present to whatever they believe is their truth. We will expand on this skill as we learn about living in a space of observation versus evaluation in Chapter 7: Honest Expression.

THE BRAIN IS A HOUSE!

In their book, *The Whole-Brain Child: 12 Revolutionary Strategies to Nurture Your Child's Developing Mind*, Siegel and Payne-Bryson (2011) talk about the brain using the metaphor of a house. They describe the downstairs as where the necessities like breathing, heartbeat, and temperature regulation live. Our emotions (i.e., the limbic region) are housed here, too. They describe the downstairs system as being a fully furnished part of the house. The upstairs, our cerebral cortex, is where our executive functions, reasoning, and language live. It is also where our emotional regulation develops. They describe the upstairs part of the house as under construction with tools lying about. Table 2.1 is helpful in displaying the differences between upstairs and downstairs brain functions.

Table 2.1: The upstairs and downstairs brain

Downstairs brain (bottom-*up*)	Upstairs brain (top-*down*)
Flight/flight/freeze response	Sound decision making and planning
Autonomic functions (breathing, blinking, instincts, etc.)	Balanced emotions and body
Sensory memories	Self-understanding/reflection
Strong emotions (fear, anger, excitement)	Empathy
Acting before thinking	Morality

Source: The Whole Brain Child Workbook: Practical Exercises, Worksheets and Activities to Nurture Developing Minds (Siegel and Payne-Bryson 2015, p.35)

When we want to connect with a person, we need to ask the question, "What part of the brain are they in right now?" We need to meet them where they are. If a child is in the downstairs brain and we are trying to connect with them via their upstairs brain functions and those functions are not available to them, it won't work. We need to meet them where they are. Siegel and Payne-Bryson (2011) back this argument (p.44):

> Think about what this information means, practically, as we raise kids who don't have constant access to their upstairs brain. It's unrealistic to expect them always to be rational, regulate their emotions, make good decisions, think before acting, and be empathetic—all of the things a developed upstairs brain helps them do. They can demonstrate some of these qualities to varying degrees much of the time, depending on their age. But for the most part, kids just don't have the biological skill set to do so *all* the time. Sometimes they can use their upstairs brain, and sometimes they can't. Just knowing this and adjusting our expectations can help us see that our kids are often doing the best they can with the brain they have.

Greene (2008) explains that children's and adolescents' challenging behavior stems from expectations exceeding the cognitive skills they either don't have or can't access at the moment. Greene is referring to what Siegel and Payne-Bryson (2011) called the upstairs brain. When we continue to see student behavior as purposeful or even believe that students are in direct control of their challenging behavior, we ignore the developmental aspect of their behavior. They can't use control systems that have not been developed yet.

In helping us change our view of the behavior of our secondary school students, Siegel (2013) discusses in his book *Brainstorm: The Power and Purpose of the Teenage Brain* how, during the adolescent years, the *house* is getting a remodel. He talks about how, during a remodel, some of the previously working systems like plumbing, heating, etc. go offline while new systems are introduced. We often see our students' behavior as insensitive, or lacking in thought, or even cruel. During the remodel of their brain, the upstairs brain systems are not always online at the moment. This may cause the fight or flight systems to fire up as if a threat is there. When those systems do come back online and the young person can reflect on their actions, we need to be there for them. Often those reflections bring guilt, shame, regret, or embarrassment and they sometimes need our support to work through that. Also, during that adolescent period, the emotional brain (the limbic system) is almost adult size, while the pre-frontal cortex is still child size. This means that adolescent humans have emotion systems the size of a mountain bike with the braking system of a tricycle. This leaves adolescents saying things they don't mean, acting in ways they regret, and feeling embarrassed and ashamed afterward.

TRAUMA

Trauma is not the events we experience; it is our response to these events. It lives in our central nervous system as part of our stress response. In all respects it is a dysregulated nervous system. It is our response to events that surpass our nervous system's ability to cope with abuse, bullying, loss, neglect, pain, witnessing or experiencing violence, and even systemic issues like homophobia, poverty, racism, or other forms of discrimination.

The categories of trauma are natural, man-made, or historical. Natural disasters include large-scale flooding, hurricanes, chemical spills, wildfires, earthquakes, or even nuclear accidents. They can also include house fires, long-term power outages, or a tree falling on your house. Examples of man-made trauma include combat trauma, neglect, physical trauma, rape, sexual abuse, and war. Historical traumas include gender violence, genocide, homophobia, racism, and slavery.

Trauma has been shown to impact gene expression, which has become the newly growing field of epigenetics (Burke-Harris 2018). Intergenerational trauma is more mysterious and harder to see. It is the theory that individuals and families pass traumatic responses down from generation to generation by way of changes in DNA. It is also transmitted through the narratives and coping behaviors passed down from generation to generation. We can pass down changes in cortisol that impact our health.

Trauma becomes developmental when it impacts the growing brain of children. A single event, either man-made or a natural disaster, can be traumatic for a child (even an adult) when they witness or experience death, loss, and grief, or a sense they have lost all control of the world around them. This could include rape, accidents, hurricanes, or school shootings. These events would be referred to as acute traumatic events. Chronic trauma is when the events are repeated and ongoing, such as sexual abuse, neglect, domestic violence, or even war. In 2011, children and adults in New Zealand experienced repeated aftershocks following an earthquake. This happened again in Puerto Rico in 2020, where the trauma of an earthquake was repeated over and over for days on end as aftershocks kept coming.

Secondary trauma is when individuals become traumatized by being exposed to other people's trauma. This can happen to first responders such as police, ambulance, or fire workers. It can happen to emergency room personnel after repeatedly being exposed to victims of accidents or murders. This concept clicked for me when I learned about a psychiatrist who had been having nightmares about being in Vietnam during the war. The issue was that he had never been in the armed forces and had never been to Vietnam. He was experiencing the symptoms of his patient's trauma. It can also happen to educators who are exposed daily to children in distress. Educators are susceptible to vicarious trauma when they display the symptoms of trauma in response to repeated and prolonged exposure trauma that isn't theirs. For educators, coming to school each day and repeatedly seeing children suffer from trauma-related stress can take a toll on an educator's well-being.

TOXIC STRESS

Stress, in and of itself, is not negative. Our nervous system is stressed when we are hungry, tired, and bored but those things don't tend to send us into a fight or flight mode as our nervous system has evaluated them as non-threats. Our stress response system is designed to continuously scan for danger and threat. Even while asleep, our subconscious mind is working to keep us safe. Tiny sounds in the night are being evaluated by the stress response systems of the brain to determine threat or no threat. Have you ever woken suddenly in the night feeling hyper-alert and panicky? It may be your brain's acute stress response system kicking in. Typical physiological symptoms of a stress response can include:

- Heart rate may increase.

- Eyesight becomes narrowed (tunnel vision).

- Surge of adrenaline.

- Surge of cortisol.

- Surge of natural opioids (the body's pain relief).

- Non-essential bodily functions, such as digestion, decrease.

- Increase in breathing (rib cage expands to take in more oxygen).

- More oxygen-rich blood is sent to limbs to either run or fight.

- Loss of hearing.

- Blood sugar increases.

When a threat is identified, the lower parts of the brain (the downstairs) begin to respond. Essentially what is happening is that the downstairs brain is taking over and a variety of things may occur physiologically while the cognitive parts of the brain (the upstairs) begin to go offline for a while. The downstairs brain is the part of the brain where fight, flight, freeze, faint, or fawn responses occur. Fight is when our brain is going to face the threat. Flight is when we are going to get out of the way of the threat. Freeze is when the brain determines we need to remain perfectly still to almost trick that threat into thinking we are not there. Faint is when the brain decides the best response is to play dead. Fawn is appeasing or when the brain has us befriend the threat. Examples of how stress responses show up as behavior in the classroom are provided in Table 2.2.

Table 2.2: Examples of stress response behaviors

Fight	Flight	Freeze	Fawn
Aggression	Walking/running out of class	Blank stares	Perfectionism
Arguing	Ignoring	Disassociation	Over-preparing
Threats	Head down, hoodie up!	Numb (shrug)	Overly helpful
Silliness	Cutting class	Head on desk	Befriends bullies
Defiance	Leaving school	Refusal to answer questions or follow commands	Submits to pressure easily
Yelling	Hovering	Appears forgetful	Lacks boundaries
Hitting/biting/spitting	Purposely getting kicked out	Inability to move	Exaggerated people pleasing
Cursing/vulgar language	Withdrawing	Exhibiting numbness	
Sudden outbursts	Daydreaming	Inability to recognize familiar faces	
Posturing	Seeming to sleep	Avoids tasks	
Pacing	Headphones or earbuds		
Provoking adults	Mindless cell phone surfing		
Throwing objects	Hiding under desks, tables		
Talking back			
Slamming doors or lockers			
Hands in fists			
Refusal to sit at desk			

Source: Adapted from Caplan (2015, slide 6)

Situations of life and death or threat of emotional or physical harm that come into play bring about our fight, flight, freeze, or fawn response. Constant and prolonged exposure to trauma can leave people in a constant state of stress that keeps an individual's nervous system in a heightened level of awareness for longer periods of time (Burke-Harris 2018; van der Kolk 2014). It means people can stay in the downstairs brain with less or little access to the upstairs brain in these types of situations. You could look at it as chronic dysregulation. Jim Sporleder and Heather Forbes (2016), authors of *The Trauma-Informed School: A Step-by-Step Implementation Guide for Administrators and School Personnel*, speak to this in a way that may resonate for those of us working in education. They say (p.20):

> When children have prolonged experiences of adversity without a caring adult in their lives, the result is toxic stress. Their bodies remain in activation mode (fight-flight-freeze). Stress activates the body's physiological response with increased levels of stress hormones. Normally, higher levels of stress hormones are essential to our survival. However, excessive exposure to stress is harmful because the body continues to pump out high levels of stress hormones which then become toxic to the body. The cumulative result of this over-activated stress-response system in the context of chronic adversity is what is known as toxic stress.

WHAT ARE ACES?

Adverse childhood experiences (ACEs) are potentially traumatic events that occur in childhood and can severely impact development, health, well-being, and opportunity. The original ACEs study, a collaboration between the Centers for Disease Control and Prevention (CDC) and Kaiser Permanente's Health Appraisal Clinic in San Diego, was initiated in the late 1990s and examined data from 17,337 adults (CDC 2019). All ACEs questions asked respondents to refer to their first 18 years of life and the purpose was to examine the link between childhood stressors and adult health. The survey contained a series of ten questions about adverse childhood experiences (e.g., physical, psychological, and social issues) the individuals may have been exposed to growing up. The ten questions focused on:[1]

- abuse
  - emotional
  - physical
  - sexual
- neglect
  - emotional
  - physical
- household dysfunction
  - mother treated violently
  - household substance abuse
  - household mental illness
  - parental separation
  - incarcerated household member.

An individual's ACEs score is the total sum of the different categories of ACEs reported by participants. Including ACES Too High (www.acestoohigh.org), there is a plethora of data, data summaries, and research studies that document the outcomes from the ACEs study (CDC 2019; Middlebrooks and Audage 2008). A summary from the original study shows that, while there were differences between males and females, 26% of the participants reported at least one ACE score, nearly 16% reported a score of two, 9.5% reported three experiences, and 12.5% reported a score of four or more. Among all respondents, 64% reported at least one ACE. According to the CDC, the higher the ACEs score, the greater chance an individual will experience adverse health behaviors (e.g., smoking, substance abuse), a wide range of chronic health outcomes (e.g., cancer,

---

1   Adapted from www.cdc.gov/other/agencymaterials.html. Reference to specific commercial products, manufacturers, companies, or trademarks does not constitute its endorsement or recommendation by the U.S. Government, Department of Health and Human Services, or Centers for Disease Control and Prevention.

diabetes, heart disease), maternal and child health concerns, financial concerns, teen pregnancy, and work-related problems (e.g., absenteeism, unstable work histories). The effects of ACEs can be passed on to children. Some children may face further exposure to toxic stress from historical and ongoing traumas due to systemic racism or the impacts of poverty resulting from limited educational and economic opportunities. Toxic stress from ACEs can change brain development and affect such things as attention, decision-making, learning, and response to stress.

TRAUMA-INFORMED SCHOOLS

Our starting point when working with students exposed to toxic stress and trauma must be finding a place and a way to keep them safe from re-traumatization and prevent further dysregulation of their stress response. While this seems like an insurmountable task on the surface, it is doable. Once we have considered what part of the brain our young person is in that we are connecting with, whether it is the upstairs or downstairs, the preference is to put judgments to the side. We must consider the possibility the person we are trying to connect with is fighting a battle we know nothing about. This is especially the case when thinking through behaviors that make no sense to us.

For most students in our immediate classrooms, we are talking about complex developmental trauma. Complex trauma is when a child or adolescent is experiencing multiple layers of trauma in their lives simultaneously, perhaps living through neglect, sexual, physical, and emotional abuse. This is the type of trauma children experience when coming from foster homes that didn't meet their needs, living with alcoholic parents, having undiagnosed mental illness, or there being poverty where they live perhaps with no access to food or electricity. This is, for example, the boy whose parent was arrested last night, and he was sent to foster care with adults he doesn't know. Or this is the girl who puts her head down on her desk with her hoodie up, earbuds in, and tries to catch up on the sleep she didn't get last night because she was up listening to her parents fight and she could not complete her math homework. How could she? She has no quiet place to do it and, in comparison to the other stuff, math seems unimportant right now as it has nothing to do with survival.

According to ACES Too High, over 35 million children in the USA have experienced one or more types of childhood trauma (Stevens 2013). Young people living with trauma may be challenged because their brains tend to be stuck in stress responses, either hyper-arousal or disassociation. It means their stress response system is on super-alert all the time. For this reason, our responses to their behavior need to be trauma-informed—calm and non-punitive—and this is best found in well-executed restorative dialogue after they have had a chance to calm down and is why we do best to use calm tones and restorative dialogue in a restorative culture. Boyes-Watson and Pranis (2015) write in their book *Circle Forward: Building a Restorative School Community* (p.8):

> A trauma-sensitive learning environment is one in which a child feels appreciated and cared for by adults at school; the classroom and school environment is emotionally and physically safe; and clearly articulated standards for behavior are reinforced through positive interventions and relationships with adults and peers. We believe that healing from trauma comes from the reliable and repeated experience of supportive and healthy relationships.

I consulted in a school where these ideas were being implemented. There was one adult in the building who didn't yet really understand what being trauma-informed meant. He would call students out publicly in the halls for being out of uniform, using a raised voice. He would use a tone of judgment for students whose dress didn't meet the dress code. There are three concerns with this:

1. **What was said?** When calling out the student in a trauma-informed climate, adults would be saying, "Wait, we don't know why he is out of uniform." "It could be that mom was too drunk to do laundry." "Could be a parent was arrested and the kid was taken into foster care last night?" We don't know what has happened to the student that we can't see. We need to follow the rule to "ask, don't tell."

2. **Using a raised voice and judgmental tone:** If that happens at home and is followed by beatings or other harsh punishments, raising your voice at a child could be sending them into fight or flight; or worse, into a dissociative state of freeze or faint.

3. **Calling a student out publicly:** This is the double standard between

how we treat adults versus children and youth. Had he done this to a fellow adult, there may have been a fight or a union grievance.

This same adult thought nothing of stopping a class in the middle of a lesson to publicly talk to a student about their behavior which, often, was not that disruptive. This teacher would interrupt the lesson to tell students to sit up or put something away. On more than one occasion, these tactics took moments that could have been de-escalated but drove the situation to the point of dangerous confrontation with a combination of a raised voice, loss of control, and public shaming.

In our classrooms, acute stress-responses may look like bad behavior, a child who is deliberately not meeting expectations, or even aggression. Our conventional thinking is to assume the student isn't trying hard enough or motivated to meet the expectations. Our conventional thinking may also lead us to believe that the student is either trying to get out of something or trying to get something. It is more likely a child with a trauma history trying to get something, and that something is safety. They are also trying to get out of something—their perception that they are in danger. While you and I may not see any danger, a trauma-impacted child can be stuck in a place where their perception is that the world is a dangerous place.

So how does this downstairs brain stuff show up in a classroom? Fight looks like fight: talking back, throwing punches, biting, hitting, etc. Except, sometimes fight also leads to giggles or silliness. This is because of the serotonin boost we get when our brains think we need to care about the threat. This mood uplift to care can lead to giggles. You might be one of those people who, as a child, got the giggles when you got a talking-to from an adult. This happens not because children are not taking things seriously; it happens because they *are* taking it seriously.

Flight shows up in ways that seem obvious, like running out of class or hiding under desks. It can sneak past us when it looks like bad behavior when a teenager is wearing earbuds or headphones. Some students will use earbuds or headphones as a way of blocking out auditory sensory information they find overwhelming. They may not even have music playing. Wearing earbuds and headphones can also send the message to others of *leave me alone* or *don't talk to me*. Another way flight behavior shows up is hovering. Picture the student who is talking a mile a minute and it seems that they are just making up reasons to talk to you, to be around you, and are closely following you around the room. This is flight behavior. This student may be running away from something and has grounded themselves in safety near you. Stop whatever you are engaged in and give your presence to this child. They may need co-regulation.

Toxic stress and resultant trauma also show up in other ways. For some teens, their reactions to triggers are disproportionate to the events. We might give a simple reminder of the expectations and get cursed out as a response. This disproportionate response is because the young person's brain is perceiving our words as threats even if they were not intended that way. Some of that may be a result of the re-wiring and reconstruction of the brain during the teen years. It also may be a response to trauma.

Trauma is also another reason to avoid using threats of punishments. As the brain becomes more stressed, the availability of the neocortex to perform executive and regulatory functions becomes limited as well. This frontal part of the brain is where cause and effect thinking, impulse control, and emotional regulation live. Without access to those processes, young people under the added stress of the threat of punishment do not have the emotional control to stop or pull themselves back in the face of the threat. The more of a threat we use on a child, the more stressed they become; and the more stressed, the less control. Stressed-out children may not be able to think clearly enough to have control of their behavior; in fact, it just stresses them out more as they try to control themselves and can't. It's a vicious cycle for children with trauma.

Trauma expert and prolific writer, van der Kolk (2014), writes in his book *The Body Keeps the Score: Brain, Mind, And Body in the Healing of Trauma* (p.280):

> It is much more productive to see aggression or depression, arrogance or passivity as learned behaviors: Somewhere along the line, the patient came to believe that he or she could survive only if he or she was tough, invisible, or absent, or that it was safer to give up. Like traumatic memories that keep intruding until they are laid to rest, traumatic adaptions continue until the human organism feels safe and integrates all the parts of itself that are stuck in fighting or warding off the trauma.

EMOTION IS CONTAGIOUS

Another thing worth adding about stress is that it is contagious. Our emotions are contagious. We have all been in a room full of laughter, when in walks a certain person and, suddenly, the mood in the room changes. We have all seen how our classrooms change when just one person is added or subtracted. We all know that one person can light up a room with their smile and another person can change the dynamics to doom and gloom with their energy.

Our stress levels as adults impact the students around us. They are looking to us to help give them a sense of safety. When they sense we are stressed out, their nervous system reacts to our stress. When they sense our anxiety, they become anxious with us. Even if you think you've put the best smile on you can, it won't help. The brain's stress-response threat-detection system doesn't tend to fall for tricks. Dysregulated adults will dysregulate young people with trauma in their history, and maybe even the ones without any trauma in their history.

I consulted in one school that had been under physical reconstruction for the previous three years. The unsettling nature of having education happen in a construction zone was dysregulating for both students and staff. To compound this, the reconstruction project had not been completed enough to allow for sporting events or school plays. Many of the primary ways the school created community were also blocked by the revamp of the building. This left limited ways to create relationships and community within the school.

This school seemed to have an unusually high number of adults working who had also attended that school as a student, and the third year of reconstruction was the same year the original parts of the building disappeared. It was like ripping the carpet out from underneath them. It was taking away what the adults, for decades, had seen as a secure base. The place they had not only attended school and the place where their primary livelihood was found was now literally gone. I am not sure the staff could see in themselves just how much that was impacting them. For students, it was a similar sense of losing the secure base of the place they had been learning in for years.

The stress was putting everyone on edge. It caused teachers to be short and snappy with students. Students were short-tempered and talking back to the adults. No one had the normal level of frustration tolerance they might have had. This led to all sorts of behavior challenges in the school. It became a vicious cycle of teachers being stressed by students' behavior, and students being stressed by their teachers' stress. I saw that everyone seemed to be feeding everyone else's stress.

This lack of calm and community in the school created a toxic emotional space. Both staff and students were dealing with their own stress while simultaneously feeding each other's stress. Add to that the stress students were bringing to school from their own traumas, and there was a recipe for disaster. Discipline referrals by the end of November had exceeded the entire number of the previous year. Students were being arrested for fighting. Teachers were complaining the school was being run by the students. One teacher said, "Discipline here is a joke."

This also brought on the nay-sayers to this work. They wanted the administration to get *tough* on behavior issues. One teacher referred to restorative and trauma-informed work as "lipstick on a pig" and touted how we need to come down on the behavior. I was always surprised by this teacher's reaction, as not enough restorative practices had been put into place for it to even be considered "lipstick on a pig" or anything else for that matter. This teacher exclaimed loudly how restorative wasn't working, despite the fact we had only just begun the implementation.

Our positivity and calmness are also contagious as well as our compassion and empathy. The more supportive and calm we become as staff, the more students become calm and feel safer in our presence.

UNIVERSAL PRECAUTIONS

A helpful concept for creating a trauma-informed school is an approach called universal precautions. In the world of infectious disease, standard universal precautions are taken to prevent its spread. These include wearing gloves, washing hands, and wearing masks and surgical gowns. The idea behind universal precautions is to assume that all body fluids are contaminated with something communicable and that we take all precautions not to spread that contamination.

To create a trauma-informed school, we use the same idea. Since we may not know who in the school is living with the impacts of trauma, we treat each child (and staff member) as if they have. We make it standard protocol to follow precautions. We assume that every child that jumps up and runs out of the classroom is seeking safety. We make it standard that we never hug someone without asking them if it's okay to touch them. We don't yell unless there is a safety concern and, even then, we are attuned to the fact that yelling could trigger negative behaviors.

Trauma keeps young people in their downstairs brain, unable to get upstairs and access more executive functions where learning happens. For some students that safety is hard to come by. Trauma impedes learning. By using calm and respectful approaches such as restorative practices as a standard precaution, we give students a better chance at learning, because the environment is safe, consistent, stable, and supports them rather than threatening them with punishment.

Part of universal precautions needs to be co-regulation. We, as adults, need to do our best to be calm and regulated, especially if a student becomes dysregulated, because they react to our stress and our calm. If we are talking about a child living in a fight, flight, or freeze mode, they are looking to us to feel safe. This is modeling; if we want to teach our children self-regulation, we also must model self-regulation.

Our new response to young people, as a part of universal precautions, needs to be steeped in the Relationship Matrix, as explained in Chapter 1. We need a better ratio of boundaries versus support and care. We need to stop trying to solve problems unilaterally using power-over tactics and demand, and instead move toward a more collaborative and proactive way of problem-solving. Some examples of universal precautions include:

- Ask and request consent before touching people or being touched.

- No yelling.

- Avoid sarcasm.

- Trade praise for gratitude.

- Connect before correcting behavior.

- Give transition warnings.

- Relationships over compliance.

- No tickling.

- Avoid picking younger children up from behind. Pick them up from within their view.

Another starting point when dealing with trauma (and what I believe sums up what we have said so far) comes from Souers and Hall (2016) in their book *Fostering Resilient Learners: Strategies for Creating a*

Trauma-Sensitive Classroom. They share so eloquently at the start of their book five fundamental truths about trauma (p.10–11):

1. Trauma is real.

2. Trauma is prevalent. In fact, it is much more common than we like to think.

3. Trauma is toxic to the brain and can affect development and learning in a multitude of ways.

4. In our schools, we need to be prepared to support students who have experienced trauma, even if we don't know exactly who they are.

5. Children are resilient, and within positive learning environments they can grow, learn, and succeed.

So, what does a positive learning environment look like? It starts with us moving from the question "What's wrong with you?," which always seems to provoke alphabet soup like attention deficit disorder (ADD), attention deficit hyperactivity disorder (ADHD), oppositional defiant disorder (ODD), obsessive compulsive disorder (OCD), etc., and asking the question, "What happened to you?,"[2] which we hope invokes compassion and empathy.

The hope is that this book has stressed just how much a force of calm we need to become for our students. The first step in the art of connection is connecting with ourselves. Our mindfulness practice will provide us with many of the skills of nonjudgment and non-reaction that we need to be the force of calm. While we will dive deeper into the practice of mindfulness in Chapter 5, part of our job becomes co-regulation of the student's stress response, and again we can't put an oxygen mask on others unless we have put one on ourselves first. We must learn to regulate our own stress response in tough times. So far, many of the teachers I have met who embody this work in their hearts have already mastered the concept of co-regulation. They can calm the toughest of students and see past behaviors to see a kid "in-struggle" not a kid "in-trouble."

---

2   Sandra Bloom (1997) refers to this in her book *Creating Sanctuary: Toward An Evolution of Sane Societies* (p.191) as follows: "Our program director (Joe Federaro) said it best when he observed that we (the Sanctuary program) had stopped asking the fundamental question 'What's wrong with you?' and changed it to 'What has happened to you?'"

We need to be committed to the embodiment of principles, values, and foundations of the work of restorative laid out in Chapter 1 of this book. Trauma-informed and Restorative Justice is not about what we do; it is about who we are and who we choose to be when we show up. What I have also learned is that showing up is half of it. Being fully present at the moment is the secret of connection with other human beings. Paying attention to our own sense of resilience is also helpful in modeling it for students and fellow staff members.

STRATEGIES FOR CONNECTION

What follows are strategies for connecting with students who have behavioral challenges. Each strategy can be used by itself or in coordination with another. You probably have dozens of strategies you already use in your practice of building relationships with young folks. If there are strategies you already have in your toolbox, compare each with the suggestions listed below.

Strategy 1: Look for needs

Needs were discussed in Chapter 1 as a motivating factor for human behavior. Everything we do is motivated by one or more underlying universal human needs. It doesn't matter what gender you are, your age, or where you live on the planet, we all have the same basic universal human needs and we are all doing our best with the strategies we use to meet those needs.

Universal needs are never in conflict. Conflict lives at the level of the strategies we use to meet those needs. When we find the most life-enriching strategy for everyone's needs to be recognized and valued equally, we also manage to leave people seen, heard, and valued. Sometimes needs cannot be met. Even when needs cannot be met, just to be seen and validated as a person with a need is sometimes more important than having a need met.

Marshall Rosenberg's work on Nonviolent Communication (2003a, 2003b, 2015) leaves us with a sense of hope that we could have that world. A world where we talk in a language of needs. A world where feelings were not a source of blame, and they become the traffic signals of our needs. A world where we look at a student's behavior, stop, empathize with their feelings, and say to ourselves, "What need is Billy trying to meet and what is behind that need?"

Step 1: Connect with your own needs and feelings

As part of mindful living, we want to be present with ourselves. Not only do we want to be aware on an intellectual level, we also want to connect with our feelings on a whole-body level. Pay attention to your emotions and the sensations in your body (e.g., experience the tightness in your chest).

Learning to read body sensations is an important aspect of connecting body to and with brain responses and may be helpful in trauma recovery as trauma can leave a huge disconnection between body and brain. Body scans are useful in mindfulness practice. We can train ourselves to be aware of and connected to our bodies and learn to listen to the messages our body sends to us about our needs. In my workshops I talk about strengthening the parasympathetic (calming) responses with practices such as yoga, meditation, and mindfulness.

In *Being Genuine: Stop Being Nice, Start Being Real*, author and humorist, Thomas d'Ansembourg (2007), talks about how our feelings are like the dashboard of a car. A car's dash has lights and gauges to tell us what is happening to the car. The dash clues us in on what the car needs. A service engine message or light means the car is due for its regular service (e.g., an oil change or spark plug replacement) or indicates there is a minor problem with the electronics or engine that needs attention. When the gas light appears, it is telling us that the fuel is almost gone and the car needs gas (and likely soon!).

Our emotions are the dashboards of our life and do the same for us. Feel fully the frustration, joy, anger, love, and hunger that make up the dashboard for your life. When we feel hungry, it can be assumed we need food or comfort. When we feel scared, it's our body's way of telling us we need safety. When we feel lonely, it is our body telling us we need connection. By staying connected and present to our body sensations, we can stay connected to what drives us—our universal human needs. And this helps us to recognize the needs of others, sometimes in surprising ways. Remember to always bring yourself home to your breathing. I once heard that our breath is the steering wheel of our lives.

Step 2: Connect with others (i.e., empathy)

Finding our calm with other's behaviors means we must first recognize the needs behind the behavior. This does not need to be done out loud; we can do this just for ourselves. Empathizing with others, especially with children and youth who have been exposed to traumatic events, can be so eye-opening because it can acknowledge the needs behind the behavior. The student under the table is now seen for their need for safety. The individual who just cursed you out is now seen for their need to be heard about their anger, fear, or shame. The student who is getting into a power struggle with you has a need to dominate. Needs are what they are. We all have them. There are no good or bad needs; just needs. Needs humanize us.

Strategy 2: Connect before you correct

In the spring of 2017, at the first annual Trauma-Informed Schools Conference, Jim Sporleder spoke about his time as Principal of Lincoln Alternative High School in Walla Walla, Washington. He offered three steps for handling behavior that was showing signs of fight, flight, freeze, or faint. Let's look more closely at each step. You'll see that none of the steps involves stickers or suspensions. There are no rewards or imposed suffering in these steps. Just connection!

Step 1: Drop the mirror (nothing is personal)

We have been telling teachers for years to not take classroom behavior personally. In the real world, it hurts to have a student, in whom you have invested hours and hours, respond with an expletive after you offered a simple hello and a smile. It is incredibly disappointing to have a student sleep through what you thought would be an energizing and fun lesson plan. Not taking it personally is an art and a practice. It is also an essential element when dealing with behaviors. While young people can be empathic and considerate at times, they are still egocentric and, more often than not, they are only just learning how to process and respond to a pretty complicated world. We are all doing the best we can at the moment we are in with the skills we have.

When we start seeing the world through a trauma-informed lens, we truly see why it is important to follow the words of wisdom to be kind to everyone we meet, because everyone is fighting a battle that we may know nothing about. When I was in India during the summer of 2014, I learned about an idea of karma that I like: "What other people may do to you is their karma. How you respond is yours." Even if it was personal, you do not have to respond in kind with an eye for an eye. The most effective way to stop an argument is with understanding. It is almost impossible to continue arguing with someone who is, at the same time, trying to understand you.

Step 2: Co-regulate the dysregulated

We need to focus on stress levels for both staff and students. We need to know about the different forms of stress and how we can help co-regulate the stress levels of those around us when others fail to be able to do it themselves. No one person can handle their stress all of the time. We all have moments where this life seems too much to handle. That is part of the human experience. If stress becomes toxic, it may be because there is no buffering adult or person to help us regain our sense of control and safety.

As part of universal precautions, we want to operate from a place where all stress is possibly toxic and where stressed-out students might need our help in co-regulating their stress. We need to start by putting our own oxygen mask on first. If we are not being mindful of our own stuff, we are not emotionally available for the children or adults who might be *in-struggle* around us.

Next, we need to focus on the human being in front of us. Don't worry about the behaviors. For each student, focus on *how* not *what*. How might you support them in their present struggle? This will not be perceived by the student as rewarding bad behavior, because we know in this approach there is no bad behavior. For the student, he might be trying to meet a need and the strategy used did not work out. It wasn't bad or good; it was either regulating or dysregulating for this individual.

Regulation of our stress starts with the awareness we are stressed (i.e., mindfulness). This is something many people living with trauma don't recognize in themselves. A disconnect happens between the brain and the body. While this tactic doesn't seem productive to most of us, the disconnection from feelings makes tons of sense when you see it through the lens of trauma. When you are in danger, either emotionally or physically, it makes sense that our brain would shut down our feelings to protect us. This helps us to understand why some children and adolescents when in stress play it out like they are fine although they are not. They genuinely don't always know they are stressed, especially when being stressed is almost the baseline starting point. How would you know that you are stressed out if being stressed is your normal?

Our focus becomes checking in with children to find out what is happening to them. Jim Sporleder, in the film *Paper Tigers* (Pritzker, Scully and Redford 2015), asks students, "On a scale of 1–10, what's your stress?" When hearing them answer with 7 and 8, he understands that their language processing is compromised and their ability to calm themselves is also compromised, or they are using calming techniques that work for them, like pacing, punching, yelling, or smoking pot. It means their breaking point is closer and their window of tolerance is getting smaller and they are doing everything they know to stop themselves from breaking. The key is that they are doing everything they know how to do. Since developmental trauma impacts the healthy development of cognitive skills, it is likely they don't have the skills that others have. Once we know their stress is high, our job is to bring it down before we do anything else. There is nothing else worth doing in those moments. This can involve any number of strategies, starting with an adult who can stay grounded and supportive.

This is probably a nice place for a warning. Once you truly open the door to listening to stories, asking what's behind the stress, you'd best be ready to hear what you're about to hear. It could be some tough stuff. Please see Chapter 6 on empathy and Chapter 11 on restorative language to tune up your skills on what to do next. Just keep in mind that you need to be the force of grounding and calm support, and not the controller of behavior or the source of further suffering (i.e., punishments).

Step 3: Build relationships

Relationships matter for those in-struggle and those not in-struggle. It is likely the relationship that has helped those not in-struggle to not be in-struggle! All young people have a deep desire to be in a positive, life-enriching relationship with others. We are hardwired for connection. It is painful for us to not be in connection. We crave it. We search for it. We heal because of it. Be sure when you build relationships with students that the foundations are built on common humanity, not just academics. Students need to know who you are before they can trust you. They need to connect to your humanity, not just your teaching. Talk to them about their favorite Pokémon, their favorite sports figure, their love of cooking—all the while also allowing them to hear about your love of your dog or your love of books. Have lunch with a student, attend their sporting event, take an interest in their interest. Invite them into yours. Share your favorite music with them, talk to them about your favorite books, read the stories that were read to you. As you continue through this book, we will explore even more ideas about how to build and maintain relationships with students.

Strategy 3: Check the physical environment

We need to be mindful that those affected by trauma may be either overly tolerant of stress or super-sensitive to it. We want to make sure the physical environment is not a source of more stress or a trigger for a fight-flight response. Too much sensory information from the environment can be just as triggering as too little—students may be starving for sensory stimulus or their senses may not be able to take in too much sensory information. Our classrooms need to be mindful of that. Too many decorations or neon-bright classroom wall colors might be over-stimulating.

Overall classroom climate

While it may sound awkward, think of a spa. Warm or earth-tone colors, warm and inviting lights, solid colors as opposed to patterns, and quiet.

Clutter

Be sure there is no clutter. Piles of books, papers, supplies, or just stuff lying around in chaos will feel like chaos. Clutter may provide more sensory information than a child exposed to trauma can handle. Clutter can bring on anxiety in anyone! We want organized classrooms with materials in bins or baskets made of natural materials. We want things labeled with words and pictures if possible. Supplies and materials have their place, and it may take our modeling to help teach students how to maintain this organized space. Keep wall posters and decorations, including bulletin boards, to no more than two-thirds of the wall space (Sorrels 2015).

Lights

Classrooms and administrative offices within our school buildings are often filled with bright, white fluorescent lighting. For some exposed to trauma, this can be an overload of sensory information and over-stimulating. Work the lights in the room to help students regulate their stress. Use as much natural light as you can, with an ability to control it as well. Using blinds to block out light or bringing in light when needed can help regulate emotions and moods. Also, be mindful during nap times for younger students. Dimming the lights can be triggering. Provide nightlights and glowsticks, and allow smaller children to take their naps near a table light.

Noise

Sound can soothe or irritate any of us. I love heavy metal music when I work out at the gym, yet that same music would irritate me later in the evening. Children can be the same way. Playing some softer mood music before class begins or during nap time can be a way to help regulate moods. Try also to be mindful of the sounds we introduce and how they impact children with trauma in their history. Loud sounds like fire drills or even the chimes we use to get students' attention can be enough to dysregulate any student for hours. It is also important to connect the dots. If we have a fire drill or lockdown drill and, immediately afterward, we find a student struggling with challenging behaviors, the noise and student's struggle might be related.

Pay attention to other sounds (e.g., air-conditioners, fans, and open windows) that can get in the way and cause competition in the ability to hear. A child who comes from a tough place may have difficulty separating all the auditory sensory information. They may want to listen to what is being said by their teacher or classmates but can't get past the competing sounds. These sounds may also just add stimuli to a nervous system that is already overstimulated, and that might be problematic. On the flip side, it may be that the student is accustomed to chaos and noise and is now placed in silence. This, too, can alert the nervous system if the environment is out of a child's norm. It can be important to recognize that nap time, quiz time, or quiet reading time may be uncomfortable for a child when their nervous system interprets that quiet as a threat.

Scents

Our olfactory sense is closely connected to our memories. This helps us to understand why we think of certain holidays when we smell specific foods. We may even connect smells of perfumes to people we knew who wore those scents. In our classrooms and school spaces, we want to limit the use of strong scents. We also want to be aware when strong scents are present and that a student's behaviors may be a reaction to a certain smell. This is especially true for teachers when their classrooms are located near the cafeteria or other food preparation area, as the smell of food can be a trigger for some students if food has been unavailable to them or denied as a punishment. Many teachers and, even trauma-informed practitioners, suggest using diffusers with relaxing scents in the classroom. My concern about using scents in a classroom is that it may serve as a trigger for a student if they were abused in an environment that contained that same scent.

Seating

For students who may be dysregulated, different types of room set-ups and arrangements for seating can be important. Some desks and seats in schools are very uncomfortable. Imagine what that is like for any person when they need to spend an entire day in those seats. Allowing different types of seats (e.g., bean bag chairs, couches, or standing desks) so that students feel comfortable can be a way to calm hyper children down or wake sleepy children up. Also, be mindful about changing these things around without warning students. Especially for our children coming from foster care or who may be homeless, changing the room set-up can be a trigger of negative experiences.

Clocks

Crazy as it sounds, clocks can make a difference to a child who has been exposed to trauma, causing some to lose their ability to manage or process time. They can struggle with "How long is ten minutes?" or even the concept of waiting. Having working clocks that accurately tell the time and that students can read can help alleviate stress. In addition, it is valuable to have a schedule for the day that offers predictability of when things will happen and at what time.

Bathrooms

Trauma can have significant impacts on a developing child's interoceptive system. This is the sense in the body that tells humans when they are thirsty, hungry, tired, or need to use the restroom. Some children impacted by trauma struggle to interpret the messages their body is sending them. They may not realize they need to use the restroom or wait until the last minute. They may go to the restroom, thinking they need to only to find they don't, then ask to go again just a short time later. They may struggle with constipation issues because they don't read the signals their body is sending about needing to go. Teachers and staff may interpret this behavior as trying to get out of class or work when it could be a student trying to figure out the messages their body is sending. Other students may have issues around separation anxiety and using the bathroom. They have fears of being alone while they go. Children who have been sexually abused may have issues around their genitalia that make bathroom issues embarrassing or awkward. One last note: The hormones and chemicals involved in the fight-flight-freeze response also have the side effect of making people need to urinate. Nervous adults and children tend to need the toilet in response to anxiety or fear. We need to be mindful as our younger students take care of their body's needs that we don't interpret their struggle as bad behavior.

There is always more to know about trauma and its impacts on memory, learning, behavior, and health. The field of studying trauma and its impact on development is fairly new and unfolding at a rapid rate. This chapter does not go into the depth this topic requires; it is the start of your journey and you will need to dig deeper. As we conclude this chapter, the thought we will end on is this: Trauma is a growing and emerging topic in the world of restorative practices. Adding the trauma-informed lens to our work means that every program, every activity, every lesson plan, every movie choice needs to be filtered through the lens of being trauma-informed. It needs to guide how we set up a policy and a procedure, as well as guide our relationships with parents, students, and fellow staff members. Remember that a trauma-informed school is also a trauma-informed workplace.

Chapter 3 will help us to unpack the four elements of a trauma-informed restorative school. We will look at changing our language from one of disconnection to one that fosters relational ecology. We will explore the value of building relationships and how to repair those relationships when they are damaged.

The Four Elements of a Restorative School Climate and Culture

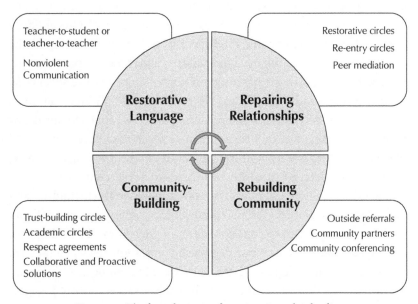

Teacher-to-student or teacher-to-teacher

Nonviolent Communication

Restorative circles

Re-entry circles

Peer mediation

Restorative Language

Repairing Relationships

Community-Building

Rebuilding Community

Trust-building circles
Academic circles
Respect agreements
Collaborative and Proactive Solutions

Outside referrals
Community partners
Community conferencing

Figure 3.1: The four elements of a restorative school culture

An important consideration of restorative is the question about how we are going to reshape the school climate and culture to fit this way of being. Restorative in schools has four main elements that build a culture of connection: restorative language, community-building, repairing relationships, and rebuilding community. All these elements require problem-solving and conflict resolution. When we solve problems that are at the root of the behaviors, problem-solving is both preventative and reparative. In this chapter, we explore the important elements of a restorative climate and culture and the various ways we create brave spaces where equity and inclusion can be discussed. Let's look at these elements.

RESTORATIVE LANGUAGE

We use restorative language in our one-on-one conversations and our interactions with colleagues, so we can model what connection looks like, sounds like, and feels like to our students. Restorative language allows us to talk in ways that live out our values. There are things adults believe are okay to say to children and youth and in ways that we would never speak to our fellow adults. Adults who wake up on the wrong side of the bed and act a little cranky toward co-workers, spouses, or friends are likely to get a pass when they say, "I'm just having a bad day." Our children and youth, on the other hand, rarely get that pass. If they wake up on the wrong side of the bed and speak to adults from that cranky space, they get scolded for being disrespectful or, even worse, adults may use adversarial power-struggles with them: "What did you say to me?" "Watch your tone, mister!" "Who do you think you're talking to?" If we spoke to our fellow adults in the same way that we sometimes speak to children, we would likely have a dozen more conflicts. Somehow, we believe it is acceptable, if not appropriate, to speak to children and adolescents using tones and words that we would never use with adults. We teach children and adolescents about respect through modeling and being respectful of them.

It is also important to consider the timing when we are talking with children and adolescents. Trying to reason with someone when they are in a state of fight or flight is useless—they are in their downstairs brain. The neural networks in the brain that they need to access are not engaged, and the networks that are engaged won't help us. We are better off using regulating, calming, and de-escalating tactics when trying to reason.

A communication practice useful to deescalating a situation is Nonviolent Communication (Rosenberg 2003b, 2015). In his book *Nonviolent Communication: A Language of Life*, Rosenberg (2015) talks about just how much our words are a language of blame and judgment and how Nonviolent Communication is a language of connection. Rosenberg notes that in our norm, we use communication to get people to do stuff. Rosenberg suggests we make the goal of communication simply connection. Of course, that begs the question, what do you mean by connection? Brené Brown (2010), in her book *The Gifts of Imperfection: Let Go of Who You Think You're Supposed to Be and Embrace Who You Are*, defines connection as "the energy that exists between people when they feel seen, heard, and valued" (p.19). My experiences as a mediator have confirmed this idea as I have felt that moment when people feel seen, heard, and valued in the mediation. The tension leaves the room. Feet cross over legs, and shoulders drop to relaxed positions. A connection with others can be almost magical.

In trying to explain life-alienating communication in her book *Nonviolent Communication Companion Workbook: A Practical Guide for Individuals, Group, or Classroom Study*, Lucy Leu (2003) refers to our communication breakdowns as the "four Ds of Disconnection" (p.66)— namely Diagnosis, Deserve, Denial, and Demands. You will find there may be overlap between the terms. For example, often the element of what one deserves is tied to a diagnosis. Next, we will examine each of the four Ds of Disconnection.

Making a diagnosis

We are skilled as humans in telling each other what we are instead of connecting with what we need, and we do so when we use terms like unruly, misbehaved, quiet, etc. We use judgment, comparison, and evaluation of each other, which so often make it less likely our needs will be met. Calling a student disrespectful isn't likely to make them want to show us respect.

Using deserve language

The deserve words we use can also be used to justify violence and harm. We have been raised in our punitive world to believe that good people deserve our praise and rewards and bad people *deserve* to suffer. We celebrate the bad guys getting what they deserve, often without the compassion of asking what happened to them to put them where they are. When we label children and adolescents as being good children and adolescents, it implies that someplace there are bad children and adolescents.

As humans, we have come to put things into little boxes, such as good, bad, right, wrong, or even trash versus treasure. These words are often far too simplistic to describe the complex shades of gray that exist in the world around us. It seems we only need slightly more information and what we once thought was good becomes bad and what we thought was trash is now a precious treasure. Often, we rarely have all the information we need to make those choices. There is always the lurking chance that another sliver of information will change our minds.

In his work around Choice Theory, Glasser (1998) believed this right and wrong dichotomy was a source of much of the world's misery. He writes (p.5):

> The simple operational premise of the external control psychology the world uses is: Punish the people who are doing wrong, so they will do what we say is right; then reward them, so they keep doing what we want them to do. This premise dominates the thinking of most people on earth. What makes this psychology so prevalent is that those who have the power—agents of government, parents, teachers, business managers, and religious leaders, who also define what's right or wrong—totally support it. And the people they control, having so little control over their own lives, find some security in accepting the control of these powerful people. It is unfortunate that almost no one is aware that this controlling, coercing, or forcing psychology is creating the widespread misery that, as much as we have tried, we have not yet been able to reduce.

In another example using the concept of what others *deserve*, reflect for a moment on a study by Bandura, Underwood, and Fromson (1975), "Disinhibition of Aggression through Diffusion of Responsibility and Dehumanization of Victims." The research methodology led a team of researchers on a series of experiments that would label participants in three categories: humanized, dehumanized, and neutral. The humanized group was described to participants as perceptive and understanding, whereas the dehumanized group was described as an animalistic rotten bunch. The control group participants were not described at all.

In one of the condition groups, the subjects were told that each of them was assigned supervisory responsibility for a member of the decision-making team and they personally determined the level of shock the supervisee would get. They had three groups of decision-makers who would each be tricked into thinking they overheard a discussion they were not supposed to hear from those running the experiment that painted each group as humanized (perceptive and understanding), dehumanized (rotten and animalistic bunch), or neutral. What happened to each of them is telling.

The neutral group was shocked with moderate amounts and moderate intensities. As one would almost expect, the humanized group was shocked less and at slightly lower intensities. Also, as one might expect, the dehumanized, rotten bunch were shocked the most and at the higher intensity. Why? Easy—the dehumanized group were labeled as the bad guys.

When you stop to think about this study, just by painting a group as bad or rotten, we are willing to harm them more. Vice-versa, when we paint a group as good, we don't want to harm them. Now think about students when we suspend, punish, or expel. How often do we want them more severely punished, based on how much we have judged them as bad children? How often do we punish children and youth more harshly because our implicit bias tells us negative labels about their race, sexuality, or gender? Look at the experiences of any group during history who were painted the bad guys and you might also see the group subjected to the hate crimes of that time. Bandura *et al.* wrote in the final discussion of their paper:

> The uniformly low aggressiveness at the outset and the differential escalation of punitiveness under different feedback conditions indicate that the dehumanizing procedures produced their effects by divesting the victims of their humanness rather than through social sanctioning of punitive actions. In everyday life, of course, dehumanizing practices are almost invariably accompanied by active encouragement and reinforcement of maltreatment of those who are victimized. (1975, p.267)

Our words are powerful!

The idea that things are either right or wrong isn't always helpful when teaching students. This seems surprising to most educators. Yet, we can teach without ever telling students they are wrong and still be effective teachers. If a student presents with the incorrect solution to a math problem (e.g., 2+2=5), telling them that they are wrong isn't as helpful as getting them to explore the correct answer. The teacher could respond by saying, "When I add 2+2, I get a different answer than you. Could you explain to me how you came to this?" Encourage students to think about their thinking, rather than offering a judgment of their answers.

It is not that right and wrong do not exist. Right and wrong do exist. It is just that living our lives only believing what we know as right or wrong is not helpful. No one will ever truly know what is right from wrong for themselves or anyone else. We can know what will meet our needs and the needs of others, so why not invest your energy there instead?

Denial

Rosenberg (2003b, 2015) discusses how we use language to deny choice and responsibility. We deny responsibility for our actions by using language to attribute our actions to things outside ourselves. It is a way of denying we had a choice, and we also do the same to others. We use words and phrases like "have to," "must," or "they made me" to deny choices we have in any given circumstance. Rosenberg listed a few of the ways we use our language to attribute our responsibility to outside forces, and I have added a few of my own observations:[1]

- **Gender roles:** "Women have to…"

- **Our role or position:** "I am the teacher and I have to…" "I am the principal here, so I have to…"

- **Other people's actions:** "I had to suspend him because he refused to…"

- **Our diagnosis or condition:** "I have to have my coffee, it's an addiction."

- **Group pressure:** "I only give out behavior bucks because the other teachers do."

- **Authority figures:** "I only apologized because Ms. Smith made me."

- **Rules/institutional policies:** "We have a zero-tolerance policy."

- **Mysterious forces:** "I don't know what came over me, I couldn't help myself."

- **Religion/belief:** "It's the Christian thing to do." "I am not judging you; the scripture is."

---

1   Adapted from Rosenberg, M. B. (2015) *Nonviolent Communication: A Language of Life* (3rd ed.), p.20. While this not an exact quote and has additions from me, I want to acknowledge this source. I changed the examples to be more education-specific.

- **Duty/obligation:** "It's what's expected of me." "It's what a good friend does."

Add to this denial of choice the word "should," and you will have a sure way of telling others their choice isn't the right one, because they "should" be doing something different that you think is the "right" choice. This word has got to be one of the more violent words in our language as it fuels our anger toward ourselves and others. An easy way to make yourself angry is to think of all the things you believe others "should" be doing for you right now. Telling people how they "should" be doing things assumes you know what is right for people.

Better yet, make a list of all the things you believe you "should" have done in your life by now. To use this word on ourselves is to say our best wasn't enough. It is shame-based. "I should have done this" or "I should have done that" screams the message that failure is unacceptable rather than a learning opportunity. Simply changing the word, "should" to "I would have liked" adds compassion to such a rigid world.

It isn't hard to see how disconnecting responsibility and choice from one's actions can be a slippery slope into finding ways to justify the things we do to other people in both ways that meet needs and ways that do not. It is also not hard to see how this disconnection can become a way of justifying actions of violence by saying "I had to do it" rather than admitting to the choices we have. Rosenberg (2015) writes, "The most dangerous of all behaviors may consist of doing things 'because we are supposed to'" (p.140).

We might also want to re-examine our thoughts about compliance from students and how much compliance is teaching them to do things disconnected from their own choices. When we raise compliant little people, we end up with compliant big people, and our history books are filled with how destructive that thinking can be.

DEMANDS

If we saw demand language in the negative, it would mean talking about how demands back people into corners and how this can engage fight, flight, or freeze triggers in our brains. The technical term for this is reactance. It is how a person behaves when perceiving a threat to their freedom. Reactance comes from humans wanting to protect their freedom and personal choice. The theory says that the more a person perceives a threat to their own choices, the more they will assert their wishes. In school terms, this means that the more we push students to do something, the less they want to do it. So why do teachers and school staff make demands for compliance with students when the science shows us that this is least likely to get compliance?

Wouldn't you much rather spin this into the positive to talk about how honoring choice, freedom, and autonomy are essential in creating a connection? For starters, if we are following the theory that all behavior is needs-based, it also means acknowledging that power, autonomy, choice, and freedom are important needs for human beings. Saying that power is a need tends to evoke scary images of dictators and high-powered CEOs who relentlessly seek power at the expense of others. Power, however, is neutral. The Dali Lama has power. Hitler had power. It is all about how we use our power. Nonviolence at the core is about using power with people rather than over or under them.

Rosenberg (2003b, 2015) says that there are only two responses to a demand: submit or rebel; we submit out of the fear of punishment or the promise of reward, and we rebel out of spite or power. As much as I would love to agree with everything he ever said, I don't know that I still agree with this one. I think we choose to submit for several complicated reasons, one of which may simply be altruism. Yes, we were given a demand; and no, we didn't feel we had a choice (even if we did). We choose to submit because we see it's in people's best interest, or that it will keep the peace, or in some cases because we think it will give us an upper hand later.

If we are going to use language as restorative dialogue, we must keep our eyes on the goal of connection. In the end, the words matter and the intention behind those words matters so much more. In the skills section of this book, we will explore how to use language to build connections rather than cause defensive reactions or escalate situations.

COMMUNITY-BUILDING

We use community-building strategies to build brave and trusting relationships that allow for learning. There is a need to do relationship-building to have a truly restorative school. This includes building the relationships between teachers, between teachers and students, and between students, and between the administration and all the above.

This is relational ecology. It utilizes team-building activities, morning meetings, class meetings, faculty meetings, town hall meetings, mentoring programs, and student-led activities. It also includes making teachers and administrators more available to connect with students and each other. It means students and staff getting used to being in community with each other. Community-building is one of our main goals in implementing restorative in schools. The idea is to create a culture where we don't need to respond to behaviors, because everyone understands how to solve problems. Circles can be an important part of this. We can use circles to allow students to get to know each other. We can use them to build socio-emotional learning skills such as emotional regulation and problem-solving. We can use them academically to enhance learning. Ultimately, we want to build a school that has a sense of community. We also build community by making sure that administration, faculty, and staff are there to greet students in the morning. Checking the students' faces, looking for anyone who looks worried, concerned, tired, or stressed. It is checking-in with those students or just making some connections.

REPAIRING RELATIONSHIPS

When relationships are harmed or fractured, we turn to our restorative practices toolbox for repairing relationships. This can be as simple as using the circle process to address harms, peer mediation to address student conflicts, or using the circle process to welcome students back after a suspension. It may involve mediations or restorative chats using restorative questions. In our conventional wisdom, student behavior has long been viewed as being between the teacher (the keeper of behavior) and the student (the misbehaver). In restorative, we see behavior as a break in the social contract of respect that involves the classroom as a community. No longer is that a break in the rules, it is a harm against our community. We will go into more detail on how to facilitate these circles, as well as expand our ability to use restorative language, in Chapter 14.

REBUILDING COMMUNITY

We also need to stay connected to our partners in the community to help us when the big stuff happens, so that we have connections when rebuilding the community when circumstances or harm seriously impact us. In a restorative school, we hope that it becomes rare that we will need to rebuild broken relationships when trust and community have been violated. It is during times like this that it helps to bring in the larger community to circle up. We invite parents, coaches, pastors, or even police officers to come in and help us repair the harm as a community. We want to be able to support students while still holding them accountable for any actions they have taken that have caused harm. This can include referrals to local mental health agencies, to community service opportunities, and even to our faith communities when applicable. We will talk more about how this process works in Section 3.

Congratulations! You have made it through Section 1, which hopes to shift the lens through which you see children's (and adult's) behavior—even your own behavior. The hope is that you see how punishment and reward systems can be replaced with support systems that still hold children accountable for creating harm while supporting them in their effort to be human. Next, we will dive into Section 2 where we will explore the Five Skills of Restorative. Once we have changed the lens on how we see behavior, we need to put new things into practice and that takes a new set of skills that have the potential to deepen our new view on our children.

— SECTION 2 —

THE FIVE SKILLS OF RESTORATIVE

— CHAPTER 4 —

The Five Skills of Restorative

In the movie *The Karate Kid* (Avildsen 1984), a young man named Daniel is being harassed by bullies. He seeks out the help of a neighbor, Mr. Miyagi, to teach him how to defend himself using karate. Reluctantly, Mr. Miyagi agrees to take him on as a student. He starts Daniel off by having him wax a parking lot full of cars using a special technique of "wax on, wax off." He follows that by having him sand the deck of his house with another technique using big circle movements with his hands and arms. He follows that with several more chores, including painting a fence and painting a house. There are specific ways for doing each task.

After several weeks, a tired and angry Daniel explodes at his teacher, with accusations of being used as a slave. He demands to know when Mr. Miyagi will start teaching him anything about karate. Mr. Miyagi says to Daniel, "Show me how to sand the floor." Daniel, being a defiant young man, mockingly shows Mr. Miyagi how to sand the floor, waving his arms in circles and making mocking noises. Mr. Miyagi quickly corrects Daniel and guides him into making more perfect and slow circles with his arms. Miyagi then says, "Show me 'wax on, wax off,'" and again Daniel waves his arms around while making mocking sounds. Mr. Miyagi patiently corrects him, guiding Daniel's arms and hands into making the right moves. This is repeated to paint the fence up and down and paint the house side to side, each time with Mr. Miyagi correcting Daniel's form and motion, making sure the boy has mastered each skill. Mr. Miyagi then asks Daniel again to show him "wax on, wax off," this time throwing some punches, which Daniel skillfully blocks while looking totally amazed with himself. He does the same for "paint the fence," where Daniel surprises himself with what he is now able to do. This is repeated for each skill, showing Daniel how he had been learning karate all along; he just didn't make the connection.

During the following five chapters, we will focus on each of the five main skills essential to being restorative. It is important to note that restorative is less about what to do and more about who to be. That is why a change in heart is the starting point and the skills come next. While a paradigm shift and the change of heart are the biggest requirements for making restorative work, specific skill sets are needed as well. Learning each skill can feel a little bit like Daniel learning karate—perhaps frustrating and at times seemingly impossible. Yet it is doable. The connection to the restorative practices isn't always evident at first.

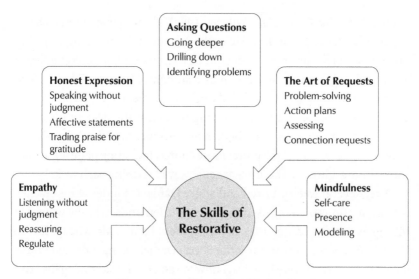

Figure 4.1: The Five Skills of Restorative

— CHAPTER 5 —

Mindfulness

Mindfulness is an often-misunderstood term. In restorative, we want that term to be about being aware or awake in the present moment. It means being present with each thought we have, each feeling we experience, and each action we take. It is fully taking in life's richness as it happens, without judgment. It's about not getting to the bottom of a bag of chips and saying, "Oh, I ate that whole bag" and then feeling guilty and sad we didn't enjoy each chip. It's about pulling into the parking spot at work and not remembering the drive we just took. How many of us have driven right by the exit we were supposed to take, only to realize our mind was not in tune with our actions? We were someplace else.

In his book *Peace Is Every Step: The Path of Mindfulness in Everyday Life* (1991), Thich Nhat Hanh, a Vietnamese Buddhist monk known for founding "Engaged Buddhism," describes how mindfulness is like doing the dishes. If we are living in the future moment, thinking about drinking our after-dinner tea, then we are not thinking about the warm soapy water, the feel of the plates in our hands, or the care that is needed so we don't break a glass. Our minds are anxious to get to our tea. We may rush washing the dishes unaware of whether we really got them as clean as we would like. Most importantly, we don't take the time to enjoy the moment and live it.

We need to learn to be present to ourselves, so we have the capacity to be present to the other humans with whom we come into contact. Mindfulness goes beyond the cushion of meditation practice or the mats of yoga practice. We do best to practice mindfulness day to day and moment to moment. This means to be mindful with our eating, mindful with our seeing, or mindful with our listening. Mindful being is the difference between mindfulness as something you do rather than something you are. We need to *be* in a state of mindfulness.

We also need to stay mindful when we are thinking about discipline. In our conventional thinking, punishment gets dished out with this myth that punishment must fit the crime. The reality is that this means the desire for punishment reflects how angry we are at the person who has wronged us. Rarely does this mean we are thinking about what the person will learn from the punishment we are dishing out. We tend to focus on either showing others how serious the offense is or how much it has angered or shamed us.

It might be timely at this point to enlarge a little on the concept of shame and how it can trigger unhelpful behaviors that impede our capacity to move toward more effective responses, particularly when young people are non-compliant and disruptive. It may also explain some of the emotional and behavioral responses by young people when they are shamed. While in this chapter on mindfulness there is no room for a detailed explanation of the psycho-biology theory[1] that explains these issues, in a nutshell, shame, once triggered (in an adult or a child), creates a kind of "social pain." This indicates that there has been an impediment which blocks our interest in, and/or enjoyment of, what is happening in any moment. This is painful enough for the adult or child to have developed defenses to cope, unless they have the skills and knowledge to understand what is happening to them, and to manage their responses. This is especially the case for adults and children who have suffered toxic stress and the associated trauma. Shame is often masked by anger, and this makes it a little harder to discern.

In the classroom or playground, when a child does not meet our expectations, it blocks our interest and enjoyment in the lesson or activity, and this can trigger shame in educators. It's not that the teacher thinks, "I've done something to be ashamed of," rather, they think, "My students should be compliant," and the immediate response is one of feeling diminished, or possibly, incompetent. This triggers one of the typical behavioral responses to shame: "Attack other." Hence, the desire for punishment, designed to show the young person who is the boss and who has the power. If we are not aware of our responses, or have no skills to self-regulate, there is little chance that we can use our "upstairs" brain to make more effective decisions about what to do next. If we took time to

---

1   A more detailed explanation of affect and script psychology and how it applies to restorative practice is available in Kelly and Thorsborne (2014).

think more critically about the punishments, we might see that they don't teach what we want, and that often they teach the opposite.

To avoid these first emotional responses from overtaking us, it is helpful to build our own pause button. This is not an easy task and requires practice. This prevents those moments where we feel the regret the second the words leave our lips. It gives us a moment to check in with ourselves to be sure we really are acting on the best intentions we have for our children and youth. And it might give us time to examine our own needs. If we follow a Nonviolent Communication approach to our language, then these needs can be expressed in more curious, nonjudgmental ways, instead of shaming and punitive ways.

We have all either been on a plane or seen in movies where the flight attendant says, "Should there be a sudden drop in cabin pressure, an oxygen mask will fall from the ceiling. Please affix your mask before helping others." This is the same philosophy we need with being restorative. We just aren't that much of a support to others if we are not supporting ourselves. Developing our pause button using mindfulness means learning to be alive and present in the moment. John Kabat Zinn developed Mindfulness-Based Stress Reduction (MSBR) as a form of meditation, body awareness, and yoga designed to reduce pain and assist in a variety of other medical issues. The practice is focused on a mindful awareness of our body and a routine of learning to focus our attention. It means learning what we can and can't control. It means that we have zero control of other people's actions or behavior.

DEVELOPING A PAUSE BUTTON

In the book, *Getting More Out of Restorative Practices in Schools: Practical Approaches to Improve School Wellbeing and Strengthen Community Engagement*, Annie O'Shaughnessy (2019) introduces us to P.A^2.I.R. This is a powerful mindfulness practice of pausing, especially before we engage with students. Let's look at the steps:

- **Pause:** Before engaging with a student about their behavior or incident in our classroom, we need to get grounded, so we are a force for co-regulation not punishment. Being grounded also means we can stay connected to our own pre-frontal cortex and not be hijacked by our nervous system's stress response. It means responding rather than reacting. This can be done simply through breathing and allowing our attention to go to our feet connecting to the earth below us. Another effective strategy is to search the room for things we can see, touch, or name, even anchoring onto one for a few moments. This in-the-moment pause is best supported by an ongoing formal practice, so we have ways of grounding ourselves when we need to.

During this pause, we also strive to consciously drop the assumptions or judgments we hold of this student so we can treat them equitably and show respect for their humanity. Remember, they are *in-struggle* not *in-trouble*.

- **Assess:** Bring your attention to your own experience. What is your body feeling and needing? Do you remember in Chapter 1 where we learned to listen for our basic needs? What are yours in this moment? What is your *observation, feeling, need,* and even your *request* in the moment? Also notice your intention or goal of intervention, as we discussed in Chapter 1. Are you wanting this student to suffer or feel supported?

- **Acknowledge:** Continue from the Assess step by verbally acknowledging the student's humanity. In keeping with the spirit of "connect before you correct," take the time to acknowledge your relationship with the student first, or if you have no relationship, to acknowledge something you guess to be true for them (e.g., "Following schools rules all day must be hard" or "I bet it's hard feeling like you don't have much freedom in school"). Then you can address the issue at hand. O'Shaughnessy (2019) writes, "Begin interaction with student by acknowledging what you notice, what is observable and true" (p.149).

- **Inquire:** Keeping in mind that restorative conversations are a dance of asking questions, listening with empathy, and using honest expression, we need to drill down into what is really happening for this student. This is part problem-solving and part providing co-regulation. We may start by using honest expression: "When I notice X (observation), I feel X (feeling), because I value or care about X. Can you tell me what's up?"

During this step, note for yourself that restorative has a

toolbox. You could use the restorative questions. You could use a plan B session (explained in Chapter 13 of this book). The goal is connection with both us and the student. It allows us to tear down our assumptions and biases, and explore what is truly happening. A powerful way to affirm the student's responses so they will continue towards Restore/Repair is to reflect back what you heard them say and ask, "Did I get that right?" or "What am I missing?"

- **Restore/repair:** Collaborate on a plan to restore relationships with self, with you, and perhaps with the class. Those plans can be ways to regulate, apologize, or even solve the problems leading to the behaviors.

HOW MINDFULNESS SUPPORTS THE SUCCESS OF P.A^2.I.R

No communication protocol or script works unless we are fully present and able to access our best selves. Mindfulness can be as simple as making sure we are taking care of ourselves with compassion. Not only is self-care important to model to youth, children, and those with whom we are working, but it also gives us more control of our fight, flight, or freeze responses. It is hard to be compassionate, empathic, or loving when we are hungry, tired, stressed out, or in pain. Teaching ourselves to be aware and present to ourselves in the moment allows us to be present with others. This has been summed up for years with the simple proverb "Hurt people hurt people." When we are not taking care of ourselves or we are hurting and stressed, we are far more likely to pass that stress and hurt onto others. If we are present to ourselves with compassion rather than judgment, we are more likely to care for our needs and have compassion for our mistakes. Mindfulness means learning to be present in the moment—to be fully alive to what we are seeing, doing, hearing, and even teaching. We want to be present to ourselves, so we have the capacity to be present with others.

Find simple and doable ways to care for yourself. Take breaks, eat, breathe, pray, meditate, do lunchtime yoga, and take walks—even if you only do this for a few precious moments in the day. Avoid glorifying the culture of busy! Today it seems we wear our "busy" like a badge of honor. If the answer to the question, "How are you?" isn't words like overwhelmed, exhausted, or busy, then somehow, we are not working hard enough or hustling for our worthiness in the world. Like everything else we do, this is a message to children that being stressed out is not only okay, it is preferred. Such a message serves no one.

MODELING MINDFULNESS

We need to be mindful that we are modeling our expectations, our attitudes, our reactions, and our skills to others whether we know it or not. Can you imagine the teacher standing at the front of a chaotic classroom yelling for everyone to calm down? Maybe that teacher is you. Are you modeling the behavior you expect? Are you modeling one behavior while asking for another? If you are the supervisor who never takes breaks, works long hours, and boasts about how busy you are, a message has been sent to your employees that this is what you expect to see of them. The trouble is that tired, overworked, and rushing people are prone to make mistakes and tend to be unproductive. This same idea extends to administrators in school. At many schools, the staff seem stressed out, overwhelmed, and frustrated; then you meet the principal, who tells you, "There is no time, we're too busy." Sadly, that stress is being modeled and passed on to the students through a chain reaction. Stressed-out leaders will stress out staff who will then stress out students, especially those with histories of trauma.

When we stand at the front of the classroom and bark, yell, and use sarcasm or other signs of disrespect, we are modeling that behavior to our students. They learn how to treat each other by how we treat them and how we treat our colleagues. In one school where I was doing some consulting work with teachers, I learned that the teachers had so much conflict with one another they would interrupt each other's classes to yell and scream at each other in front of the students. We need to connect with our own emotions, so we learn to regulate them enough to model emotional regulation to our students.

In their book, *The Whole-Brain Child: 12 Revolutionary Strategies to Nurture Your Child's Developing Mind*, Siegel and Payne-Bryson (2011) reinforced this notion of children learning from what we model (p.56):

> And, of course, consider what you are modeling with your own behavior. As you teach them about honesty, generosity, kindness, and respect, make sure that they see you living a life that embodies those values as well.

The examples you set, for good and for bad, will significantly impact the way your child's upstairs brain develops.

Another popular mistake some teachers and adults make is not modeling the skill of cognitive flexibility, which is the ability to flow from one to task to another, sometimes mid-stream, or to take thoughts and expand on them. This could be demanding Danny put away his math book because we have moved on to reading. We get angry with Tanesha because she won't come in from the playground, and our response is to start dishing out threats to get her back to class. We are asking them to be flexible, which can be hard if you don't have that skill. When we demand students be flexible, all the while modeling inflexibility, don't think the mixed messaging isn't confusing—because it is. Our being mindful of our behavior, especially our reactions, is so we can model for our students what we expect from them.

Once we have developed our own practice that brings us into the present moment (whatever that may be—yoga, meditation, adult coloring books, Tai Chi, etc.) it is helpful to begin cultivating that skill in our students. This can be as simple as taking a moment of pause at the beginning of class to do some breathing exercises, or just sitting. Allow students to develop a practice with you.

Until we become present, aware, and mindful of our words, thoughts, actions, feelings, and experiences, it is unlikely we will be in a place to choose our responses rather than just respond. Mindfulness allows us to be compassionate to ourselves, awake to ourselves, and awake to the life around us.

FORMAL VERSUS INFORMAL MINDFULNESS PRACTICE

At the end of the day, mindfulness is a skill that serves no one if it is not practiced. Typically, formal practice is where we have set time aside committed to deliberate and focused work on fine-tuning our attention and awareness of the present moment. Formal practice tends to use awareness anchors where we can focus our attention. When we find that our thoughts, distractions, and other things have taken our attention away from our anchor, we gently and with kindness to ourselves bring our awareness home again to our anchor. Some examples of anchors may be:

- sounds

- breath

- body sensations

- focal points

- visualizations

- chants or mantras

- feet/body grounded to the floor

- drumming.

According to the MBSR model's *Standards of Practice* (Santorelli 2014), some examples of a formal practice would be sitting meditation, body scan, walking meditation, and even mindful eating. Informal practice tends to be how we bring the same present nonjudgmental awareness into the rest of our lives. Examples of this are mindful communication, brushing our teeth, mindful seeing, mindful driving, mindful movement, or even breath awareness throughout the day as a way of grounding ourselves as we go through our day-to-day lives. It is our formal practices that help us to be successful in our informal practices, teaching us to be more present and aware of both the pleasant and unpleasant experiences we have each day.

INFORMAL PRACTICE IN RESTORATIVE SKILLS

All the skills required to be restorative require the informal practice of mindfulness. They require us to be present to ourselves and others in the moment, aware and present to what is happening to ourselves and to others. These skills include:

- **Honest expression:** In order to connect others with the experience we are having in the moment, we need to be connected to ourselves. Honest expression isn't just about making an "I-statement." It is about expressing the experience we are having in the moment in ways that create deeper connection of ourselves and others. Ultimately, it is helpful for us to be clear with ourselves where we are in the moment. What are we feeling or needing? What are we reacting to? What would make life better? It means truly allowing ourselves to experience our feelings and connect to the needs behind them.

- **Empathic listening:** To truly listen is more than just hearing words. To deeply and compassionately listen requires us to be aware of and present to the person who is speaking to us in relationship to ourselves. We are taking in more than just words. We are taking in a person, their emotions, and their experience in the moment, and we are completely focused on them. If we are mindfully listening, we are just present to our speaker. It is not time to correct, fix, or debate their experience; it is just to be present and aware. Sometimes people need our compassion and presence, not our words.

- **Asking questions:** We benefit when we stay connected and present to the intentions behind our questions. We benefit from empathically listening to the answers. We stay nonjudgmental of person we are asking a question of when we can stay mindful and aware of our reactions to their words and how they influence our next question.

- **The art of requests:** Staying mindful to the agreements, action plans, and requests we make of each other also keeps them restorative. Do they meet human needs? Do they leave people better off than when we encountered them? Is the request doable for all those being asked? Do people have the resources to complete the requests or agreements? Even in the context of restorative practices, we need to be present and aware while in circle, while doing a Plan B session, and while mediating conflicts. We need to be aware and present to be the circle keepers or facilitators of community or family group conferences. Boyes-Watson and Pranis (2015) write in *Circle Forward: Building a Restorative School Community*: "…the Circle process itself is a mindfulness practice because it encourages participants to slow down and be present with themselves and others" (p.411).

TRAUMA-SENSITIVE MINDFULNESS

It needs to be acknowledged that mindfulness can bring up powerful feelings and sensations for both adults and children. We need to keep our trauma-sensitive lens on the skill and the practice. Trauma can leave children with some constant unpleasant sensations in their body. Even sending them into their breath can be triggering for some. Our bodies are amazing at taking care of us, and many students have developed ways to stay safe, including disconnection from their bodies and emotions. Directing their attention directly to their bodies and the sensations within can be upsetting for some. As we introduce mindfulness strategies, a suggestion may be to utilize more external anchors such as sounds or sights. As students deepen their own practices, we may be able to introduce breath, body awareness, or emotion work. This always needs to be done with some occasional check-ins with students as it may not be obvious that they are struggling. Even the quiet of the room while we meditate may be triggering for some students if that quiet is associated with negative experiences in their lives. Dimming the lights can be a trigger of past traumatic experiences. That is not to say we avoid these practices for those exposed to trauma in their past; it means staying aware and thoughtful about what is happening in the moment and what reactions we are seeing in students.

Mindfulness is both a skill and a practice. It becomes the foundational skill that supports the other four skills of restorative. We need a mindful presence to show up and stay in the moment to master the skills of this work. In Chapter 6 we will look at the skill of empathy. We will look at what it takes to listen with our whole being and offer our presence as a gift.

— CHAPTER 6 —

Empathy

Restorative requires deep listening. This is a form of listening that requires our whole person. To listen mindfully requires us to give the speaker our full presence, taking in body language, facial expressions, and tone of voice. It requires us to hear beyond the spoken words so we can hear the basic universal human needs that those words decode for us. This type of listening is also about helping to regulate dysregulated stress systems. In other words, get them (and us) out of their (our) stress response. Vietnamese Buddhist Monk Thich Nhat Hanh, while speaking in an interview with TV host Oprah Winfrey, stated that deep compassionate listening is listening in such a way as to relieve the suffering of the other person (Oprah Winfrey Network 2012).

Practitioners of restorative may find that truly listening takes some reassuring among children and youth to know that they are not in-trouble, that they won't be judged, and that things will be okay, which goes a long way when connecting. Our world today has conditioned so many of our younger generations to avoid being vulnerable for fear of judgment, punishment, or disappointment. They fear what will be done "to them" when expressing themselves, which inhibits their open and honest communications with adults. We may need to use reassuring statements that allow others to trust us, before they will say what is on their minds. This is another of the downsides of punishment: It discourages others from telling us what's really in their hearts.

The focus of this chapter is on empathic listening. We explore how mindfulness plays a role in being fully present to the person to whom we are listening. We will review non-effective strategies in communication, namely "fix-it" and "competition/defensiveness," because each gets in the way of effective communication or our ability to truly connect with others. These forms of communication keep us in our heads thinking about what we will say next. As a result, the attention of the listener is split, not present, or not mindful with the primary focus being on how to respond. As restorative practitioners, we need to listen with our whole being, using all our senses. A third, effective strategy reviewed in this chapter—empathic listening—helps us to do just that.

FIX-IT

When the story sounds as if the person is in pain, we try our best to say something that will "fix-it" to help the individual feel better. In fix-it mode, there is a tendency to want a one-sided approach to problem-solving. This, like everything else, has its place. There will always be times when offering a fix-it response may be the best choice at the moment. Indeed, fix-it can be important, such as when there are issues of safety.

When we give advice or offer options to solve problems without hearing from the other person how they want to solve a problem, they may take our advice without ever exploring all the options available to them, thereby missing the opportunity for skill development. Children often take our advice or follow our directions out of a sense of obedience or compliance. Obedient children tend not to become problem-solvers. They get trained to look to others (us) to solve problems. We are better off seeing every conversation as a chance to connect, practice problem-solving, and offer our empathy and support to each other. Children and youth don't learn to solve problems when we solve these for them or when we lecture them on what they did or didn't do. They learn to solve problems by working through real options. When we "fix-it" for them, they don't learn to do that. When we guide them through the problem-solving process, they gain vital skills and practice for later use. Table 6.1 provides examples of "fix-it" strategies.

Table 6.1: Examples of fix-it statements

Approach	Sounds like this...
Advising	"I think you should..." "Why don't you...?"
One-upping or "stacking the deck"	"That's nothing—wait till you hear what happened to me!" Or "You think you've got it bad!"
Educating	"This could turn into a very positive experience for you if you just..." Or "What did you learn from that?" Or "That's not a feeling."

Consoling	"It wasn't your fault. You did the best you could." Or "Why would anyone do that to you?"
Commiserating	"Oh, I don't like her either." Or "I feel the same way about math."
Lecturing	"I have told you a million times that this sort of behavior…"
Storytelling	"When I was your age…" Or "I know what you mean—it's just like when…"
Shutting down	"Cheer up. Don't feel so bad." Or "Don't get mad…"
Sympathizing	"Oh, you poor thing…" Or "I feel so sorry for you."
Interrogating	"When did this happen?" Or "Who was it?"
Explaining	"I would have called but…" Or "Let me explain why this happens."
Correcting	"That's not how it happened." Or "You mean last week?"

Adapted and modified from a list of the blocks to listening from Rosenberg (2015, pp.92–93)

Offering others sympathy is a variation of fix-it. When offering a student sympathy, it sounds disempowering to say, "Oh, you poor thing." Or worse yet, the sympathetic statement "I feel so bad for you" can make the person feeling bad feel even worse, rather than better.

Imagine several versions of the same story in fix-it mode. The student runs up to the teacher and says, "Johnny hit me." The teacher says, "Well, just stay away from him" (advice) or "You and Johnny are just going to have to learn to get along with each other—I just can't have students fighting in my classroom" (lecture). "Well, what did you say to him to make him hit you?" (blame the victim). Can you imagine any of those responses teaching our students actual skills with how to solve the problem?

COMPETITION/DEFENSIVENESS

There have been countless times in my work at schools where students have been sent to the dean or the office for behavior issues and the adult asks, "What happened?" and then proceeds to interrupt the students, make faces, roll the eyes, and make other gestures. I have also seen teachers reply to a student's "perceived attitude" with forms of revenge, sometimes resorting to threats. One student replied to his teacher with great irritability, declaring, "You don't even like me." The teacher replied, "You're going to think that even more if you keep up that attitude." It's moments like this where mindfulness and empathy go further in creating a connection with others. If the story is one which we disagree with or feel hurt by, we may fall into "compete" mode where we want to make the conversation a match of wits or zingers. Table 6.2 provides examples of competition/defensiveness statements.

Table 6.2: Examples of competition/defensiveness statements

Approach	Sounds like this...
Competition/ defensiveness	"You're wrong! and I am right. And, even if I am not right, I am going to prove you are wrong anyway." Or "You know that's not how it happened." Or "Oh, Mrs. Smith doesn't hate you."
Revenge	"You don't know what you are talking about." Or "Does anyone have any intelligent questions?" Or "I'll teach you to talk back to me." Or "How dare you speak to me like that!"
Silence to remain safe	"I am not talking to her till she apologizes."

EMPATHIC LISTENING

The definition of empathic listening is the ability to hear and connect with another person with such a level of connection that the listener can paraphrase, reflect back, and summarize to the speaker their feelings, needs, and the essential facts of what they have expressed about their experience. It focuses on listening to others with fully committed open-hearted interest and inquiry, without judgments or evaluations. We want to do more than just listen and reflect to the speaker our intellectual understanding of what has been expressed. Our job isn't to be able to respond with the perfect technique; it is to be present with authenticity and curiosity in pursuit of human connection.

Empathic listening:

- is not agreeing, judging, or blaming

- tells the speaker they have been heard and understood

- validates to the speaker that their feelings are acceptable and even normalized

- allows the speaker to correct, clarify mistakes, or clear up mis-understandings when needed

- offers the listener the opportunity to stand in the shoes of the speaker and gain a deeper, more meaningful connection to the shared feelings and needs experienced.

Rosenberg (2003b, 2015) gave us a formula for his take on listening. Listening isn't about how we reply; it is about how we stay present, taking in the experiences of others. It is how we capture the combination of their story, their feelings, their experience, and even the needs that are met or unmet for them. Rosenberg took the idea of empathy in communication slightly further than just active listening or reflecting back someone's words. He referred to Nonviolent Communication as listening with your whole being. He suggests we use the process of Observations, Feelings, Needs, and Requests (OFNR) when applying empathic listening. We want to connect with the experience of this person's needs as being met or not met, and the feeling that comes from that experience. When we reflect on what we are hearing, Rosenberg would suggest guessing about the needs and feelings we hear (see Table 6.3).

Table 6.3: Empathic listening

Approach	Sounds like this...
What are other people observing?	"Are you reacting to what Sally said about your paper?"
What are other people feeling and needing?	"Are you feeling disappointed because you would have liked more support preparing for the exam?"
"What are other people requesting?"	"Are you asking for an explanation of why that was said?"

For example, a student may express, with an angry tone, "You never listen to my side of things. You don't even care what I think!" In reply, we might empathize with what we heard by asking, "Are you saying you feel annoyed because you want to be heard and understood?" Below are examples of prompts and probes for empathic listening:

"Are you feeling...because you need...?"

"I am guessing you feel...because...is important to you?"

"Help me understand what you're saying."

"Let me see if I understand…"

"I get the impression that…"

"Tell me about that."

"And then what…?"

"Could you expand on that?"

"Let me see if I got this," and then summarize.

"What I heard you say is…"

To be truly empathic and present, we can employ reflective listening, summarizing, paraphrasing, empathic guesses, and even asking questions to clarify. Next, are four options that allow a speaker to know we are hearing them and exactly what it is we are hearing.

Reflective listening

We may choose to reflect on what someone said. A simple reflection involves repeating the essence of what the other individual has just said. Generally, we respond using the same words (and as accurately as possible) the speaker has used. For example, a student may say "My teacher hates me," and we might reflect by saying, "Your teacher hates you. Can you tell me about that?" We might say just a reflection without a question. For example, a student may say, "I don't like math," and the reflection is "I hear you don't like math." The intent is to *not* add interpretation or meaning to what the student has just said. Simple reflections can have profound effects on students when they hear what they have just said. This choice can be tricky with teenagers, who may see this as parroting if done too much. Younger students do seem to respond better to this, because it lets them know they were heard without too much complication. Be careful of overuse! This approach, like all listening skills, is better combined with the other skills.

Summarizing

We may choose to reflect the story back to the speaker, including as many of the important facts, feelings, and needs that the speaker expressed.

We want to be careful that we don't add our own judgments into the summary; we just summarize the facts or what we heard. Using observation language is one way of keeping our summary judgment-free.

Paraphrasing

We might just acknowledge what someone has said using similar words that show we heard something the speaker has shared with us. For example, "My boss is always pointing out my flaws and I work really hard" might get a response of "Are you saying you're working really hard and want to be seen for your accomplishments and not your weaknesses?" We are not agreeing or disagreeing with the speaker; we're just trying to acknowledge what they have said.

Empathic guesses

We may choose to stick with a more classical Nonviolent Communication response, which is to make empathic guesses about the needs and feelings we hear being expressed. When a student says, "My teacher hates me and she is always picking on me," we might respond by making a guess: "I am guessing you feel frustrated because you'd really like to be liked?" Our words don't have to be perfect and our guess doesn't have to be "right" to help us create the connection. I also think we must be aware of the age of the person we are talking to, so we can be sure not to confuse them. Asking a second grader about their need for acceptance might be better expressed as a need to be "part of the group" or "to fit in."

In Chapter 7 honest expression is reviewed. We will take time and dive into the use of affective statements and learn more about the process of Nonviolent Communication created by Marshall Rosenberg (2003b, 2015). We will learn how the dance of communication is a combination of asking questions, listening for truths, and expressing our own truths. So much of these approaches form the basis for the restorative language discussed in Chapters 8 and 11.

— CHAPTER 7 —

Honest Expression

Communication that is clear, compassionate and expresses truth without being misleading or expressing judgment is important in restorative. If you are working to implement restorative practices in your school or youth-focused organization, one of the many practices you may have learned is using affective statements. Affective statements can be a powerful way of modeling to children and youth a better way to express their feelings. Using affective statements is also a better way of pointing out behavior issues in a way that creates more connection between student and teacher. This chapter reviews some of the limitations of how affective statements are currently used and suggests an approach to how we speak to others using Nonviolent Communication created by Rosenberg (2003b, 2015).

AFFECTIVE STATEMENTS

Affective statements are often described as personal expressions of feelings in response to others' positive or negative behaviors. So many of us have been taught "I" statements, which generally follow the rule of "I feel 'X' because you did 'Y'" for some blameful reason, and here is what I really want. I am going to suggest that we use a form of "I" statements following the work of Marshall Rosenberg, psychologist and creator of Nonviolent Communication, sometimes called Compassionate Communication (Rosenberg 2015). Rosenberg would recommend that, instead of, "I because you," in Nonviolent Communication, we say "I because I."

The idea is for teachers to connect students with how their behavior is "affecting" or impacting self or others: "Using affective statements helps us to specify the behavior that a student is exhibiting and encourage or discourage that behavior while improving or maintaining the relationship between the teacher and student" (Public Counsel n.d., p.37). Many current books, toolkits, and even some workshops give examples of affective statements that sound more like blame statements than connection statements. Many sources trying to teach affective statements give examples, such as:

> "It makes me sad when I have to keep telling you to keep your arms by your sides when we're walking in a line." (Public Counsel n.d., p.37)

> "Lisa, I am frustrated that you keep disrupting class today." (Costello, Wachtel and Wachtel 2009, location 215)

> "Don, I was shocked when I graded your paper. You are capable of doing much better." (Costello *et al.* 2009, location 216)

The statements above fit the formula of stating one's feelings and then go on to explain how the feeling is the fault of the student. When we say to others that our feelings are being caused by their behaviors, it will most likely be heard as blame and fault. "I am feeling this way because of *you*" and if "*you*" change your behavior, you will "*make me*" feel better.

Children and youth need to understand that no one causes their feelings and they do not cause another person's feelings. Everyone benefits from learning that feelings are caused by needs being met or not met, and not by the actions of others. If other people's actions caused our feelings, then each time they take that action, the same feeling would come for us—except we know that isn't true. For example, on one day, a student arrives past the agreed time. This might leave us happy because we had a need for some privacy to catch up on emails. The next day, arriving past the agreed time could leaving us feeling angry because we are needing more structure in our day. Our needs in the moment bring about our feelings, not the actions of others. As Rosenberg (2015) would say, "What others do may be the stimulus for our feelings but not the cause" (p.49).

In the example above, Lisa is being sent the message that the teacher is feeling frustrated because of her actions. Perhaps the teacher is feeling frustrated because she has a need for order, respect, or cooperation from her students. It isn't Lisa's "fault" the teacher is frustrated. It is the teacher's needs that are not being met, which is the stimulus for feeling frustration.

We want students to look at their inner world mindfully, so they can learn emotional regulation. If they learn that their feelings are owned by and originate from within themselves, they can then learn to get out of the blame game. Feelings are never someone's "fault." On the other hand, if we teach them (possibly through these types of blame statements) that they are the cause of another's feelings, they are also learning the myth that others control their feelings. When you see others as the source of your pain, you increase the likelihood you will want to punish them when the feelings hurt. This continues the cycle of violence.

In the example above with Don, not only is the statement full of blame, it is also laced with a tinge of diagnosis of Don and his capabilities. If Don disagrees, this statement is likely to cause shame and disconnection, not connection. If he agrees, he will only feel disappointed rather than motivated for change. These types of statements are better than the alternative of criticizing student behavior as good or bad, right or wrong. Better still, statements can be made to be more connecting to both students and teachers. A connection- or relationship-based classroom management style could be much more impacting than the current way in which affective statements are being used in the classroom.

Restorative practices practitioners would benefit if they moved toward Rosenberg's (2003b, 2015) model of using Observations, Feelings, Needs, and Requests (OFNR) as the new and improved way of doing affective statements. The formula is simple and, with practice, will be far more effective than the typical statements currently being taught in restorative practice models. Of course, there would be a greater benefit if restorative practice practitioners combined all of Rosenberg's materials and ideas into the work they do. Beginning with OFNR is a nice first step if you are not ready in your life for everything Rosenberg proposed.

HOW HONEST EXPRESSION WORKS

Much like "I" statements without the blame, first state your observation of what you want to address, followed by your feelings about that observation. Then tack on the need that is either met or not met that is the cause of that feeling. Follow this with a request or possible strategy that may meet the need you talked about. Let's break each of these parts down a little more.

Observations

Observations are about separating what happened from the story we tell ourselves about what happened. If we want to point out to students exactly what behavior we want to address, it is best to do that in ways that don't drudge up shame, defensiveness, or resistance to our feedback. Rosenberg (2003b, 2015) suggests starting with an observation of the behavior free of judgments, criticism, blame, or diagnosis. Looking at the example above with Lisa, it is important to point out what Lisa is doing to "disrupt" the class, rather than judging the behavior as disruptive. For example: "Lisa, when I hear you talking at the same time that I am talking…" is an example of an observation. Another example from the above quotes may be "This is the third time I have seen you with your hands in the air" (an observation) as opposed to "I have to keep telling you," which sounds more like judgment.

Feelings

It is most important that we follow the words "I feel" with a word that describes physical emotions when doing affective statements. We want to model for students how to express their emotions using their words, rather than acting out their emotions in negative ways. Most of us remember our first-grade teacher saying, "Use your words," as opposed to having us act out our feelings. It becomes important for teachers to develop a strong vocabulary of *feeling* words. Be careful *not* to follow "I feel" with thoughts (e.g., I feel *like*, I feel *as if*, I feel *that you*). We also want to steer clear of pseudo-feelings. These tend to be words that evaluate or accuse others of a behavior. For example, "I feel…[insert pseudo-feeling]." Examples of pseudo-feelings include disrespected, threatened, bullied, and misunderstood. Make sure to express *your* feelings and emotions with words that express an actual physical experience that *you* are having.

Needs

It is important to follow a feeling with a need and not a blame statement about other people. We need to own our feelings, and the best way to do that is to learn to associate our feelings with the needs behind them. Our feelings act much like the dashboard in a car. Your car's dashboard has a light that comes on indicating the car needs gas; another that tells you that the tires need air. Our emotions do something similar for us. When we feel tired, it is our body's way of telling us we need rest. When we feel hungry, we most likely need food. When we feel scared, it may mean we have a need for safety. This is the best way of making an affective statement: "I feel…because I need…" This is different than "I feel because you…"

Requests

If we are going to go to the trouble of pointing out the behavior and expressing our feelings and needs, we might as well ask for what would make life more wonderful! Ask for what would meet your needs. Be as direct and clear as possible with something doable. Ask for what you *do* want rather than what you *don't* want. You cannot do a don't! Honor choice by starting with "Would you be willing to…?" Be prepared and welcome to hear "*No.*"

There are two types of requests you could make. One would be a request for action: "Would you be willing to dry the dishes while I wash them?" The other would be a connection request. We may ask others to tell us what they hear from us. We may ask others to tell us what is alive in them when they hear what we have said. We may simply ask others to talk with us about something specific.

Let's look at what these statements would look like, using the examples written in *The Restorative Practices Handbook for Teachers, Disciplinarians and Administrators* from the International Institute for Restorative Practices (Costello *et al.* 2009, location 215, 216) and then what they would look like if we used Marshall's Nonviolent Communication approach using OFNR:

Table 7.1: Revamping affective statements in restorative practice

Typical response*	Example of affective statement*	Problem with affective statement	Nonviolent Communication version
"Stop teasing Sandy."	"It makes me uncomfortable when I hear you teasing Sandy."	Feeling is blamed on student behavior and teasing is a judgment.	"When I heard you speaking to Sandy in the way you did, I felt worried because I value respect. Would you be willing to tell me what you were talking about?"

cont.

Typical response*	Example of affective statement*	Problem with affective statement	Nonviolent Communication version
"Talking during class is inappropriate."	"I am frustrated that you aren't listening to me."	Feeling is blame-based and accuses student of not listening rather than expressing a need to be heard.	"When I hear you talking at the same time I am talking, I feel frustrated because I would like to be heard. Would you be willing to raise your hand when you want to talk?"
"You shouldn't do that."	"I feel sad when you say something like that to John."	Aside from blame and accusation, there is also a bit of shame in this statement.	"When I heard what you said to John, I felt sad because I value respect. Would you be willing to tell me what you were thinking about when you said that?"
"Sit down and be quiet."	"I get angry when you talk and joke during my lectures."	Blame-based statement. Teacher's feelings attributed to student behavior.	"When I see you walking around the class and talking while I am doing a lecture, I feel angry because I really value collaboration in the class. Could I ask you to tell me how that sounds to you?"
"I don't want to see you fighting with him."	"I was shocked to see you hurt Pete."	Makes a judgment about what happened, perhaps without knowing the facts. Blames student for feeling of shock, so the teacher no longer owns feelings.	"When I saw you put your hands on Peter, I was scared because I really want safety for everyone in my classroom. Would you be willing to tell me what happened between you two?"

*Typical response and example affective statements from Costello *et al.* (2009, location 230)

To recap, our formula is simple and not entirely that different from traditional "I" statements; it is just more focused on "I":

"When I see, hear, experience…[observation]."

"I feel…[add an emotion word, not a thought]."

"Because I need, value, care about…[add a need word, not a strategy]."

"Would you be willing…[offer a strategy that will meet your need and be willing to hear 'No' in response]?"

Trading praise for gratitude

Despite the benevolent intentions and blatant overuse, praise is not a life-enriching activity nor is it restorative. To start with, it is useless feedback, because it lacks any real information. "Good job" or "Doing great" fails to inform others exactly what it is they are doing that we find so "great." How will they know to do "it" again when they don't know what "it" was? Praise is simply a verbal reward. Like most things in conventional wisdom, it doesn't do what we think it does and it doesn't work the way we think it works.

Praise can be a trigger of past or current trauma in children and adolescents. Hearing how you're a "good boy" while being abused and then hearing that from your teachers may bring about unwanted feelings and negative associations. The same can be said of other types of praise if it was accompanied by abuse.

Praise can also make challenging behavior worse for those who are living with the impacts of trauma, because it bumps up against deeply held negative beliefs that toxic stress has embedded. Heather Forbes (2012), in her book *Help for Billy: A Beyond Consequences Approach to Helping Challenging Children in the Classroom*, supports this argument (p.59):

> Billy's world has been so unpredictable and unsafe that his stability is based on his beliefs. He has to believe what he believes to survive. Giving up these beliefs would be not only scary but terrifying. He has to work to prove to the world he is "bad"; hence, compliments and praise drive him to act out even more negatively.

She goes on to further support this notion by saying that even compliments, which are a form of praise, can be unhelpful for children impacted by trauma (p.60):

> Words like "Great job, Billy, I'm so proud of you!" blatantly contradict Billy's internal framework. Messages like these are in direct contradiction to his sense of self. Newberg [Newberg & Waldman 2006] writes, "The human brain has a propensity to reject any belief that is not in accord with one's own view." Billy's entire foundation of existence can be threatened

by a compliment. He reacts not from the cognitive and rational mind that would allow good reason to accept these positive messages but from a lower state of survival. He becomes emotionally fired up by compliments. He is working to retain what is familiar and safe, even if they are negative and self-defeating. They are what is familiar and safe.

Kohn (1993) in *Punished by Rewards: The Trouble with Gold Stars, Incentive Plans, A's, Praise, and Other Bribes*, also supports this idea that praise isn't helpful (p.97):

> let us assume that our primary motive truly is to help the person we are praising. What, specifically, are we trying to do? Three goals are mentioned most frequently: enhancing performance (learning, achievement, and so forth), promoting appropriate behavior or positive values, and helping the individual to feel good about himself or herself. Over the long haul, praise, at least in the form it usually takes, fails to achieve any of these objectives and may even prove to be counter-productive.

Praise can be damaging to children with self-esteem issues. Brummelman *et al.* (2014) suggest that praising the person, but not the process, can predispose children with already low-self-esteem to feel ashamed following failure. Of course, those are the children we tend to dump lots of praise onto in our attempts at uplifting them. This again demonstrates for us how conventional wisdom isn't always what works. Inflated praise is defined as praise that has additional adjectives added, such as "incredibly" or "perfect." A simple praise statement of "You are good at this" becomes "You are incredibly good at this." The problem for us as adults then becomes "When is my praise too much or too little?" Praise is still a reward and rewards lower performance. It is an extrinsic motivator in a world where we are hoping to cultivate an internal sense of discipline. For that reason, do away with praise altogether.

Do you recall the four Ds of Disconnection we discussed in Chapter 3? Offering praise or compliments to people and/or about their work is still a form of moral judgment. It leaves us stuck in the conventional wisdom of rightness or wrongness. In a restorative school, our goal is to worry less about "what" people are in terms of good, bad, right, wrong, and more about "how" people are.

Expressing gratitude

Rosenberg (2003b, 2015) would suggest replacing praise with an expression of gratitude. Gratitude is an important part of a restorative school. It is students appreciating each other, their learning, their teachers, and the things in life they have. Gratitude can be extremely powerful and a positive influence on people's day-to-day life. When expressing gratitude, we want to use the same process we used for our affective statements of pointing out the observation. What is it specifically someone has done that we are experiencing gratitude for (i.e., an observation)? How do we feel in response to that action (i.e., a feeling)? What need has been met for us (i.e., the need)? We may follow that with a simple "Thank you."

Table 7.2: Praise versus gratitude

Praise	Gratitude
"You're doing such a great job."	"When I see you walk down the hallway without talking [observation], I feel thankful [feeling] for your cooperation [need]. Thank you!"
"Good job with the lunch line."	"When I see all 25 of you in a single file line, I feel happy to have your cooperation."
"Great job on the math quiz."	"When I see you solved four out of the five math problems, I feel so happy to see your progress and growth! Thanks for the work."
"You are such a polite young man."	"When I saw you hold the door for your classmates, I felt grateful for the respect. Thank you for doing that."

So far, we have talked about listening with empathy, and expressing ourselves honestly. In Chapter 8 we will dive into the art of asking questions. Sometimes when working with children and youth, we need to guide them as they learn to problem solve and explore incidents. Questions help us to get that clarity, break things down, and learn more about each other. We also use questions as a tool in our toolbox of restorative skills.

— CHAPTER 8 —

The Art of Asking Questions

Much has been written about the importance of questioning. In restorative, we use questions in several different ways. The catch is that questions need to come from a genuine intention to connect. To be truly restorative with questioning, one needs to see the world through the eyes of the other person and to base inquiry on empathy. In this chapter, we examine some reasons why questioning has been, and continues to be, important. We focus on why effective questioning is critical to being restorative. As we successfully address any restorative issue, questioning can be helpful in the following ways:

- **Creating connection:** If done with the right level of curiosity, intention to connect, and compassion for others, questions can be an effective vehicle for creating a connection with students or others. Questions can be the vehicle for learning about their lives, the way they process the world, or even what makes them come alive in the world.

- **Drilling down to the problem:** We can't solve behaviors. We can solve the problems that cause behavior. We need to ask questions that help us identify the problems to be solved (Greene 2014a, 2014b).

- **Identifying emotions:** Asking people how they feel can sound clinical and, at times, even condescending. Guessing someone's feelings helps when the vocabulary for emotions is either limited or unavailable in the moment. For many children, the skills for naming emotions or even expressing emotions using words may be limited or still under construction. Taking some educated guesses may be a helpful way to overcome this barrier. It can also help build those skills for them at the same time.

- **Seeking clarity:** Our questions can be a way of gaining clarity that what we think is going on with the other person is in fact what is happening. It can even be a way of gaining clarity on the words being used.

To start, we want to look at some of the various ways that questions can be used as sources of disconnection. Far too often when we are working with students to solve issues, conflicts, or problems, we misuse our questions. Here are some examples:

- **Leading questions:** When we ask questions that back the listener into an answer that we want them to say, it is a form of entrapment. Leading questions are designed to influence thinking in favor of the person doing the asking and can be viewed as a form of manipulation. They can force people into saying things they don't mean or admitting to things they did not intend. For example, "Are you done with your homework?" when you know the homework is not done. Another example would be to ask, "Isn't my way of studying better than the other options?"

- **Grilling:** This occurs when questions become more about you wanting answers than the other person having answers. The idea here is not to grill people. It is to drill down to get to the root of the issue. Grilling tends to bring up defensive reactions in humans. It can also bring up feelings of frustration when your questions impede their ability to say what they need to say, rather than what you want to hear.

- **"Why" questions:** Academically, "why" questions can be extremely helpful. In interpersonal dialogue, the suggestion is not to use "why" questions when we are dealing with problem-solving or conflicts. This is because they tend to sound accusatory/confrontational; and even when they don't sound like that, they can still be taken that way. We also already know the answers to these questions if we follow the theory that behavior is needs-based. The answer to a "why" question is always going to be "It meets needs." For children and adolescents with trauma in their background, asking a "why" question can also throw them into thinking they believe the answer they give may determine what you will do "to" them. They may become afraid or not know how to answer because they don't know what the answer will lead to. Additionally, one of the reasons "why" questions are a problem goes beyond just putting a child on the spot. In the heat of the moment or during an incident, a student may be in their downstairs brain with little access to language and executive function. "Why" questions are a demand on a function that is currently offline.

In restorative, we are best served when our questions follow some basic guidelines:

- Watch your nonverbals because your body language matters. The same question asked with the same words, yet different body language or tone can change the intention and meaning of the question. "Where is your homework?" asked with open arms and a smile is a different question when asked with folded arms and a stern look.

- Allow for pauses after a question has been asked. Some students and even adults may need time to process what you asked. Allow a moment for them to gather their thoughts and answer before nudging them to respond or asking other questions.

- Keep questions simple and avoid layering. Asking complex questions during problem-solving can be overwhelming. Try one question at a time to reduce complexity.

- Keep your vocal inflections down at the end of questions. This is sometimes referred to as "upspeak" when our vocal tone raises at the end of a sentence or statement. Doing this can make your questions sound unsure. Keeping vocal inflections on the downspeak, like you would do when making a statement, will allow your questions to sound confident yet still curious.

- Ask your questions from an authentically curious place in your heart. Don't just ask because you feel like knowing; try to have a path for your questions.

- As we discussed in Chapter 2, remember the universal pre-cautions when using restorative language. That means using calm, supportive—and more importantly—nonjudgmental tones. Our tone gives away our dysregulation and can shut communication down.

Let's look at some common types of questions that could be used to address unsolved problems, create connection, or deepen our understanding of other people's situations:

- **Breakdown questions:** These questions look at the components of a larger issue to find the challenge. For example, when a student says, "Baking a cake is hard," we might reply with the question, "Which part is the hard part? Is it mixing the ingredients, measuring the amounts, or pouring the batter?"

- **Clarification:** We could ask questions that give us deeper clarity about what was said. This could be clarity about particular words or phrases—asking what people meant by a certain word or statement. For example, "I heard you use the word 'respect.' Can you tell me what you mean by 'respect'?" Or "When you say this is taking too much time, how much is too much for you?" Or "You said respect is important to you. Can you tell me what respect is for you?"

- **Compare and contrast:** This is asking about contradictions, opposites, variations, or exceptions. We could ask why something happens under some conditions and not others. Compare questions ask for the differences between two or more things, events, or situations. Contrast questions tend to add or subtract elements to see the differences. This could be asking what a friendship looked like before and after a fight, with or without the conflict. Other examples include "Can you tell me how math class is different from the writing workshop?" or "How would your relationship be different if you were not writing partners?"

- **Empathy guess:** These questions are based in Nonviolent Communication, discussed in Chapter 7, and remind us about asking if someone is feeling "X" because they need or value "Y." While this may sound like a statement, it is still a question. It needs to be asked with the same level of curiosity and willingness to hear the answer as any other question. For example: "Are you feeling angry because you need respect?"

- **Observation of discrepancy:** These types of questions come from Greene's book *Lost at School* (2014b, p.83) and often help us to understand what is going on for a child when they describe one thing while we have observed something else. Using "honest expression" as described in Chapter 7 is helpful for these questions. For example, "When I hear you saying that you don't have any problems with Sean, and I heard you two raising your voices yesterday on the playground, I am confused and could use some clarity. Can you explain what was happening then?"

- **Relationship:** This is to do with asking about how things or people interact or their connection with each other. For example, "Can you tell me how soccer practice is related to your homework?"

- **On a scale:** A way of learning information about how something is experienced by another person, is to put it on a scale. For example, "On a scale of 1–5, how important is the science project to you?"

- **Time:** There are several different types of questions you could use regarding time. First, you could ask for timelines related to a story or problem. These give us a chronological overview of the problem. For example, we could ask for a timeline of events about the problem we are solving. We could ask about what happened first, and then what happened next. Second, you could ask questions related to the past or future. For example, "What will this mean to you in five years' time?" or "How have you solved these issues in the past?"

- **Verifying hunches:** We have all been told not to make assumptions, but as humans some assuming is just natural. It is something we do to try and make sense of things. Making assumptions isn't a problem; believing them is. Take your assumptions and turn them into curiosity. For example, if we assume that a reaction we are seeing is due to the homework, we might turn that into a curious question and ask, "Can you tell me if this reaction is related to the homework assignment?"

- **Who? What? Where? How?:** Questions such as these ask for basic information and are helpful at getting data for problem-solving or understanding events. They can be replacements for "why" questions. For example, "Who was with you on the bus?" or "Where was your backpack during the incident?"

OPEN VERSUS CLOSED QUESTIONS/STATEMENTS

In doing the work of restorative, we need open-ended questions and statements, as well as closed questions. The tendency is to use more open-ended questions when gaining information or perspective and using closed questions when creating action plans or agreements. Asking open-ended questions is a way of inviting students to talk more about their experiences. Examples of open-ended questions and statements include:

"Can you tell me more about that?"

"Would you tell me more about how that happened?"

"What are you thinking in response to what you heard John say?"

"What happens next in the story?"

"What brought you here today?"

Closed questions only seek to find a "yes" or "no" answer or a specific piece of information. Some examples of closed questions would be:

"Did she say she would do that for you?" (Asks for a "yes"/"no" answer.)

"What color was the car?" (Only seeks a specific answer.)

"Have you been fighting for a long time?" (Asks for a "yes"/ "no" answer.)

RESTORATIVE QUESTIONS

Restorative questioning (the standard questions commonly used now in a variety of schools, criminal justice, and workplace settings) was developed initially in the state of New South Wales, Australia, by a well-known pioneer of Restorative Justice, Terry O'Connell (Costello *et al.* 2009).

First used for police cautioning for youth offenders, it has been adapted by many practitioners. The questions are designed for the person responsible to explore the harm they are responsible for and to be held accountable for this. They give those impacted by the harm a space to speak about their discomfort and pain, and for all those involved to negotiate ways to repair the harm.

The questions below are adapted from *Circle Forward* (Boyes-Watson and Pranis 2015).

Exploring the incident (These questions explore the story.)

1. What happened?

2. What were you thinking about at the time?

3. What have you thought about since?

Exploring the harm (These questions explore the impact of the story.)

1. How has the incident affected you?

2. Who else has been affected? In what ways?

3. What has been the hardest part about this for you? For your family and friends?

4. What concerns you the most about this?

Exploring action plans to repair the harm (These questions explore repairing the harm.)

1. What do you think needs to happen to make things right?

2. What needs to be done to prevent this from happening again?

3. What is each of you willing to commit to improving this situation?

4. What could the agreement look like?

5. Does everyone agree with this plan?

These questions are extremely versatile in walking people through their experiences, regardless of whether they were the person responsible for creating harm or a person directly or indirectly harmed. They can be asked one-on-one or in a circle. In Chapter 14 on using circles, we will explore the various ways these questions can be used in circle or conference to help students walk through incidents of harm, current events, or even academics.

TALKING CIRCLE QUESTIONS AND PROMPTS TO DIALOGUE

We also use questions in restorative to create community. This is where we utilize our questions skills to prompt people to tell us about their lives and who they are. It is a great way of deepening our experience of each other. Circle prompts are best when the goal is to dive deeper into our relationships, not teaching or proving our points. Our questions are about deepening our understanding of each other.

For your "check-in/check-out" questions and "get-to-know-you" questions, choose questions that are meant to prompt storytelling rather than opinions. Avoid questions that might drum up controversy; opt for questions that uplift and bring smiles. For the more content-based parts of our circles, our questions can go deeper, be more controversial, and perhaps be based on current events or issues. Allow for questions that bring opinions, emotions, and even the exploration of social issues. For many of these questions, variations of the content questions from earlier in this chapter can be helpful. For example, use the clarity question to find out a student's thoughts about a subject. For example, "Tell me what [fill in issue] means to you?" You could use a contrast question to find out what would make the class more interesting. For example, "How would removing tests change our class experience?"

Check-in/check-out questions

"Compare your current mood to the weather. What is the forecast in your world today?"

"On a scale of 1–10, with 1 being a horrible day and 10 being awesome, what number are you today?"

"If your mood was a color, what color would you be today?"

"Name three words that describe your day."

"If you were to compare your day to a movie or a book, what would it be?"

"What's the best thing that happened to you today?" "What's the worst?"

"If your day was an animal, what animal would it be?"

"Give us one word to describe your mood."

Getting acquainted questions/prompts for circles

"What's your superpower?"

"Complete this sentence: 'If you knew anything about me, it would be...?'"

"Tell us a food tradition in your family."

"Tell us a song that 'moves' you."

"How did you get your name?"

"If you were a cartoon character, who would you be?"

"Describe a time when you felt like a hero?"

"You have a plane ticket to anywhere. Where are you going?"

"Who is your biggest hero and why?"

"What musical instrument would you be?"

"Share a happy memory."

"If you could have lunch with anyone from history, who would it be?"

"Share a food tradition from your family." (This could be a holiday tradition or even a weekly food ritual.)

"What do you wish adults knew about kids?"

"Name something that gives you comfort."

"Name a song that moves you."

"Name an experience where you made lemonade out of lemons."

"What is one thing people who really know you would know?"

"What is one thing you are scared of?"

"Tell us about your best five minutes of fame."

"Name something that gives you hope."

✳ ✳ ✳

In the next chapter, we will explore the art of requests. It will help us understand how to ask students to repair harm in age-appropriate ways. We will introduce restorative S.S.M.A.R.T. goals and learn how to create action plans that hold students and our communities accountable.

— CHAPTER 9 —

The Art of Requests

An often-asked question by teachers and administrators in this work is how we do "restorative consequences." This is code for punishment and suffering. It is not to say there are no restorative consequences, because there are. It just isn't what school personnel are asking for. They are asking for restorative punishments—and that is an oxymoron. In this chapter, we will explore more deeply what consequences are, what repairing harm looks like, and why we can't just have a menu of ways children will repair harm. We will learn how to create a concrete action plan that holds both our responsible youth and our community accountable.

Instead of thinking about consequences or punishments, we could think about solutions to problems. When a child blows up in the classroom, the punishment would simply reinforce their anger and frustration or worse, add to it. The consequences are that the student has impacted their relationship with their fellow students. Since nobody likes to lose their cool in front of others, I am betting the student is already ashamed and embarrassed. Asking the student if they would be willing to apologize or do something to improve relationships isn't a punishment or a consequence, it is a solution to the relationship problem caused by their behavior. Maybe we need more focus on solutions and less on consequences and punishments.

Teachers often feel "wronged" by student behaviors and look to see some suffering, so the student does not "get away with it." This is our old conventional thinking creeping back into our minds about what it means to be accountable. In our old conventional thinking, we see accountability as punishment served. In restorative thinking, accountability is about addressing the harm caused while never losing sight of the fact that, for the teacher, this is not personal. We need to put our anger aside so we can use a clear and mindful approach to the next steps that support learning discipline and not punishing. This is a reminder to drop the mirror. Boyes-Watson and Pranis (2015, p.287) write that accountability has five dimensions:

1. Acknowledging that you caused harm with your actions or behaviors.

2. Understanding how others were affected by your actions.

3. Taking steps to repair the harm to those hurt.

4. Giving back to the community.

5. Making a concrete plan so it does not happen again.

I hope that it is becoming more obvious why we can't just dish out "restorative consequences." They must be part of a process that sees accountability as addressing harm, not serving a sentence. As we discussed in Chapter 1, punishment is not true accountability and the reason is simple—punishment doesn't require any of the five dimensions, as described above, to be true. People can serve out their punishment without ever acknowledging they have harmed anyone. It is a wonder that anyone would equate punishment with accountability for this simple reason. In restorative, "consequences" need to meet the following criteria:

- **Consequences need to solve problems:** When we ask students to clean up the mess that may have been caused by their behaviors or actions, the consequence needs to act as a solution. For example, if a student broke a window, we now have the problem that a window is broken. A solution would be getting the window fixed. What role can the student play in the solution? Could the student work off the cost? Could the student learn to fix windows? Could the student work with the repair person as an assistant?

- **Consequences need to repair the harm to the community, which means they need to come from the needs and responsibilities identified by the community affected:** Consequences to repair the harm are best when they are either at the request of the person or community impacted or originate from the author of the events. They cannot be dished out by a third party unaffected by the actions. They cannot be adult imposed, or they simply become punishments.

- **Consequences also need to be age-appropriate and developmentally appropriate:** Every child is different. What we request of them and what they volunteer to do to repair the harm and atone must be doable and reasonable for their age and circumstances.

- **Consequences need to be voluntary:** If we are forcing a student to do it, the consequence is now a punishment. We are requesting that students agree to contribute to repairing the harm and that means what they do has to be done out of the energy to empathically and compassionately give, rather than out of a sense of duty or shame.

- **Consequences also need to balance the needs of the community with both the author of the action and those impacted by those acts:** This means having a consequence that enhances the lives of those impacted by the actions and the life of the person who authored those actions. It is completely fair to have those impacted ask for what would make things "right" again for them or ask for what would repair the harm.

ACTION PLANS

It may be helpful to have an action plan that is developed through a restorative process. While action plans do not always need to be formalized, at times it could be helpful to do so. Detailed plans are important, such as creating a timeline of what is to be done, by whom, and who is responsible and when will it be done (see Figure 9.1).

A useful formula to use in helping to develop an action plan is to use a S.M.A.R.T. framework (Doran 1981), a process originally developed for use in organizational management. The original acronym stood for specific, measurable, assignable, realistic, and time-bound. Since then, various people have added to, tweaked, and changed the acronym to make the model to fit a variety of circumstances. In this chapter, we are going to use S.S.M.A.R.T. This structure of our action plans helps to keep everyone accountable to each other. It also helps support keeping students within the framework of the dimensions of accountability. Let me explain each step of this acronym through the lens of restorative:

- S is for *Specific*: We want our plan to really detail what is expected of our students and the community. We want details of who, what, and how. Who is responsible for the plan? Who will monitor the plan? What are the specific actions we expect each person to commit to? How will it be accomplished?

- **S** is for *Strength-based*: What are the talents, skills, interests, and strengths of the person who caused the harm, and can those be used in the repairing of harm? If a student excels at art, could art be the vehicle of how they repair the harm?

- **M** is for *Measurable*: How will we know the plan has been completed, and how will we know everyone has lived up to the plan?

- **A** is for *Achievable*: We want to be sure students are asked to do things that are age-appropriate, doable in their particular circumstances, and have proper supports in place for the plan to be met.

- **R** is for *Restorative*: Ultimately, we must ask the question "Are we out to contribute to healing and compassion or are we seeking suffering and retribution disguised as a restorative practice?" It is vital to this work that we are honest with ourselves and each other as community members. Since so many of us have been raised in a culture of punitive thinking, it is easy to fall back to what we know to think in terms of who deserves what and how we inflict that on them. Our plan needs to be about accountability through healing and repairing, not hurting and suffering.

- **T** is for *Timely*: We do need a timeline for when things will be accomplished or met. We need to decide who is doing what and then when it will be done by. This is important, especially when we are supporting those who have been harmed or those who have caused harm in creating supports. We don't want to talk about doing stuff and then no follow through in accomplishing it.

As we create this plan, we also need to focus on the strengths and interests of a child, so we can use those to help repair the harm, seeing the student or child as a whole person and not just seeing them through the lens of one incident. This is where a student being an artist, having leadership skills, or being good at making videos can be advantageous for repairing the harm.

Action:	Due Date:	Supporter:
Action for Person Harmed:		
Action for Community:		
Action for Family:		
Action for Self:		

Figure 9.1: Restorative action plan format

The plan can be broken down into parts. How will a responsible youth repair the harm done to those directly impacted, their family, their community, and themselves? Depending on the circumstances of the event, defining how a student who created the harm will better themselves and repair harm to self is a nice starting point. Next, it is helpful to define how they will make amends or restitution to those they have directly harmed. Some might call those people victims. It is important for us to ask those directly harmed what they need to feel so that accountability or healing is possible, and then return to the responsible youth and ask if they are willing to meet those needs and how it could be done. The process is repeated for all involved.

Using the restorative questions is one way of opening the conversation about repairing harm or looking at what people need to commit to doing to bring a situation back into balance. By helping people walk through what happened, who has been impacted and how, and what needs to be done to make things right, we allow the process of healing to begin. It is helpful to ask each person what they are willing to commit to.

✶ ✶ ✶

As we reach the end of Section 2 on restorative skills, it is important to remember that these skills form the "doing" part of this work. When we couple that with the foundations and principles material from Section 1, we increase our chances that the practices that follow in Section 3 will come from a life-enriching place in us. In Section 3, we will explore how to take this new lens on behavior and our new set of skills and put them into action.

— SECTION 3 —

RESTORATIVE IN ACTION

CHAPTER 10

Restorative in Practice

There are endless possibilities of what restorative could look like in practice, because this is more of a way of *being* than *doing*. Here in this section we will look at the expanded continuum of restorative practices, starting with the most informal of practices, such as our one-on-one interactions with other humans, all the way to the formal use of conferencing. We will try to cover a few things in-between. We will also look at the history of how these practices were brought into schools.

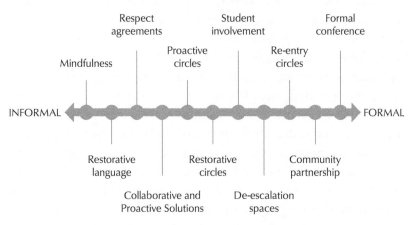

Figure 10.1: The expanded continuum of restorative

A BRIEF BACKGROUND TO RESTORATIVE PRACTICES

It is believed these practices first found their way into schools in 1994 in Queensland, Australia, when school staff at a high school were trying to address an incident of assault (Davis 2019). School staff borrowed a conferencing model being used in the criminal justice system for youth offenders that had shown promise and reworked it for students. It later expanded across Australia, New Zealand, and the UK (Thorsborne and Blood 2013). In the USA, restorative practices took hold as a response to widespread zero-tolerance policies in schools that required suspensions and expulsions for sometimes minor offenses such as having small amounts of drugs or small weapons (e.g., a plastic fruit knife) in school without bothering to explore why students had these items (Brown 2018). A non-profit organization in Pennsylvania took the Restorative Justice principles into an alternative school they were running (Evans and Vaandering 2016), out of which an international organization supporting restorative practices was born: the International Institute of Restorative Practices (IIRP).

Restorative Justice in schools, and the practices that support it, has expanded across the globe over the last 25 years. The practices have expanded from ways to respond to harm and wrongdoing to building communities that don't foster such harm. While there is little agreement on exactly what restorative practices are, there seems to be no questions what values and principles are at the heart of this work.

In the USA, this rise of restorative practices in schools ran parallel to the movement for trauma-informed schools. This movement came from clinicians and parents who were fighting for classrooms where foster children and children adopted from less-than-ideal conditions could learn. Organizations such as the Attachment & Trauma Network were leading this charge long before the term "trauma-informed" became popular. While a detailed history of the movement doesn't seem to exist, there is some notion that it was born out of models that were being used in clinical settings about how children impacted by trauma could be healed. The lessons being learned about trauma and its impacts also seem to improve outcomes for students not impacted by trauma. The idea is that we create safe learning environments and help to co-regulate student's emotions with them while building the relationships that allow them to learn. At the time of writing, trauma-informed schools and Restorative Justice in education are only just beginning to merge.

On the informal end of restorative, we use honest expression, empathic listening, and asking questions as a restorative language that creates and maintains a sense of connection and relationship with our colleagues, our students, and even parents. We use the affective questions when we need to walk through the impact of people's actions either in our own minds or out loud with a group. We use respect agreements to collaboratively work with each other and to create a sense of community where everyone has a say in how we act together. We use Greene's (2008, 2014a, 2014b) model of Collaborative and Proactive Solutions and its powerful three plans to interact with students, always keeping in mind that we have choices about how to address behaviors that are not meeting our needs and which students struggle with. All these practices start with self by being fully present to ourselves and to the practice we are engaging.

We use circle process to create, maintain, repair, and rebuild our connections to one another either with students or staff. Human beings have been using the process of sitting in circle together for generations. In restorative, we acknowledge that this longstanding tradition is extremely life-enriching.

STUDENT INVOLVEMENT

We also use mediation. Mediation helps support us by allowing a person who is outside of our conflict to use the tools of restorative to collaboratively solve problems with us. Children can be trained as neutral third parties from as young as kindergarten. In far too many schools, school staff are using mediation without the training to go alongside it. We need to be sure staff understand the role of a mediator, so we honor the best practices of mediators such as making mediation voluntary, confidential, and done by a person with no attachment to the outcome. Adults doing school-based mediation have a stake in the outcome and it would be best to acknowledge that they are not neutral third parties. Students can be trained in circle keeping for community-building circles to start, followed by training for healing circles as they grow in their skills. Students can absolutely become leaders in the trauma-informed restorative movement in schools. This marries well with social and emotional learning and community service. In schools where students need community service hours to graduate, using their service to the restorative work in their schools can be very satisfying for them and healthy for the school.

FORMAL CONFERENCING

At the most formal end of the spectrum of restorative practices, we use what is referred to as conferencing to hold the most formal of versions of the circle process. Not all restorative practitioners use the conferencing model, and some find it power-over or top-down; nor do all practitioners use circles in the way described in this book. I believe that by using the five skills described in this book, this conference process can be a valuable and moving way to address serious issues that may arise (e.g., fights, violence, cutting, truancy). When those students are returning to our communities from an absence, suspension, or re-entry from incarceration, it is vital they come back to a re-entry process that reminds them they are welcome and loved. Re-entry circles also help students set up support systems and learn what resources are available to help them succeed.

WHAT PRACTICE AND WHEN?

Restorative doesn't come with a playbook. There is no algorithm or flowchart of what practice needs to be used with what incident. All these practices must happen in the context of relational ecology. The key to both trauma-informed work and Restorative Justice is relationship. Whether or not to circle, or conference, or mediate, or chat is dependent on the main questions: What was the harm? Who was harmed? And how do we address and heal the harms? Humans don't come with a manual and nor do these practices. This book is meant to be a guide as to how these practices might serve your school, and ultimately responding to harm is best determined by those stakeholders directly impacted.

TRAINING IN PRACTICES

While it is helpful for everyone to have a basic knowledge of each practice, not everyone needs to be skilled in every practice. To start we need each person in the school community who comes into contact with children to be trained in the impacts of trauma and equity/implicit bias. We need school staff to understand the impacts of racism, classism, homophobia, sexism, and ableism (discrimination in the favoring of able-bodied people). Everyone in your school needs to understand implicit bias, oppression, and privilege, and the roles these things play in our school systems. Disproportionately, Black, Indigenous, People of Color, Lesbian, Gay, Bisexual, and Trans students are punished more often and often more harshly (Brown 2018; Davis 2019). We need as many people as possible in the school to be trained in the Five Skills of Restorative. These are the building blocks of community. It is also suggested that all staff be trained in using mindfulness practices, circle keeping, and restorative language. As we move along the continuum, classroom staff (including teachers, behavior specialist/techs, and paraprofessionals) need to know the practices that help build our classroom community (i.e., circle process, respect agreements, the restorative questions, and Collaborative and Proactive Solutions). Table 10.1 shows the level of staff training by job or role.

Table 10.1: Level of staff training by job/role

All school community	Teachers, behavior specialists, teaching assistants, paraprofessionals	Students	Administrators, middle managers, deans	Key personnel/ Restorative Justice team
The Five Skills of Restorative Justice Impacts of trauma Basics of Restorative Justice Circle keeping Mindfulness practices Restorative language Equity/ implicit bias	Restorative circles Collaborative and Proactive Solutions Respect agreements Restorative questions	Circle keeping Basics of Restorative Justice Mindfulness Peer mediation	Conferencing Re-entry circles Collaborative and Proactive Solutions	Change management Formal conferencing Collaborative and Proactive Solutions

✳ ✳ ✳

In order to create the school culture that we want, we need to pause and take a hard look at the language we use with students and each other. The next chapter will dive into just that—a language of restorative. We want to bring our school to a place where language supports the values and principles we are trying to incorporate into our community.

— CHAPTER 11 —

Restorative Language

Earlier in this book, we looked at the skills of mindfulness, asking questions, empathic listening, and honest expression. These are the basics of restorative language. The approach discussed in this chapter is an attempt to bring the skills of dialogue together, along with some additional supports to create a school-wide language that is restorative. Some readers may be familiar with the restorative dialogue/chat where we pull students aside for a private conversation. Just using the standard format of restorative questions, if done in a mechanical way, will not, by itself, deliver on real connection. It is about making sure *all* our language and words support this way of being. Restorative language asks us to rethink communication to refrain from mislabeling behaviors, and to be mindful of the words, phrases, tone, and nonverbals we use. If we can transform the language, we can also transform the culture.

You could liken restorative language to a nonjudgmental exchange of experiences. Often, perhaps through dialogue, we wish to share the experience we are having, or we want to connect with the experience others are having. When this process clicks, it is human connection. Brown (2012) defined connection as when people "feel seen, heard, and valued" (p.145). Each of us is trying desperately to connect with others and to communicate what is inside us, whether we know it or not. For some struggling children and adolescents, this may show up as maladaptive behavior. The response from others can manifest as judgment, criticism, and even comparisons. In the end, we are all trying to tell other people about what is happening in us. The experience is based in universal human needs of survival, fun, love, power, or freedom.

When this exchange of experiences happens in life-enriching and restorative ways, it can be a dance between a speaker connecting with a listener and a listener connecting with a speaker. We use honest expression to connect someone with what is alive in us at any given moment. We use empathy as a way of hearing what is alive in them. Sometimes, when others are struggling to use language to engage with us, we may use our questioning skills to find our way to their heart and what is alive there. This may include restorative questions or maybe we use other questions skills. The idea is to have a full toolbox. In some cases, this may happen to us in circle. When done in circle, this can be a powerful and healing event, with a variety of people going back and forth between sharing what is alive in them and their experience and then listening to what is alive in others and their experience (see Table 11.1).

Table 11.1: Examples of restorative dialogue choices

Student says:	Example statements:	
"I hate this class" (in an angry tone)	Honest expression:	"When I hear you say that, I feel worried because I value your participation in this class. Would you be willing to tell me one thing in particular that you hate about the class?"
	Empathy guess	"I am guessing you feel frustrated with the class because you'd like to be doing better?"
	Reflective listening	"You hate this class. Can you tell me more?"
	Questions (compare)	"Can you tell me what is different about this class compared to classes you like?"
	Questions (clarity)	"Is it the subject matter or the group work you don't like?"
	Questions (contrast)	"How would this class be different if we took the group work out?"
	Support	"How can I help?"

Often during dialogue, we get caught up on words rather than the experience behind the words. There is a whole person to connect with. A person may say, "I'm fine," while staring at the floor and gently sobbing. If we are stuck on the words, we may believe "fine" to mean the person is feeling content. If we are taking in their experience in the moment, we may make an empathic guess and ask, "Are you feeling sad [i.e., a feeling] right now because you would appreciate some connection [i.e., a need]?" Another option would be making an observation about the discrepancy (e.g., "You say you're fine—and you look really distressed. Is there something I can do to help?").

While getting caught up on words may not always serve us, it is also helpful to know that words are still powerful. It may be helpful to remove certain words from our vocabulary. There are some words we use on a regular basis (in the English language), and the suggestion is to stop using them. In dialogue, these words simply don't serve us. This is not to say these words don't have purpose; they just require intense communications skills most of us will never have. Below are examples of words and phrases to remove from your language if you want to have a truly restorative dialogue (examples of restorative dialogue choices have been provided in Table 11.1.):

- **"Should," "have to," and "must"**: These are all words that deny choice and responsibility. They are words with which we evaluate ourselves and others in negative ways. The word *"should"* (and *"ought"*) has got to be one of the most violent words in our language. It perpetuates the myth that we know what is right for others and stops us from seeing reality as it is for that person. "Should" is also the word that lies at the heart of anger. Most times when we are angry, a dialogue is happening in our heads and the word "should" tends to be at the heart. "You should be more respectful" or "You should call me more often" or "You should drive more carefully." The word drives our anger. It means the "other" has not met our expectations and has left us with needs unmet. The word "should" can induce shame, guilt, and other negative feelings. To test this theory, make yourself a list of all the things you believe you "should" have done in your life and haven't. Now, examine how you feel after writing the list. "I shouldn't have said that" or "I should have known better" or "I should dress better." I suggest the simple change of trading the word "should" for the simple phrases "I would have liked," or "I choose," or "I could." The sentence, "You shouldn't have done that" becomes "I would have appreciated it if you hadn't done that." The phrase *"have to"* or *"must"* tends to have the air of "I have no choice." Anytime we feel that our choice has been threatened or removed, we risk psychological reactance or pushback. When we use that thinking on ourselves, we often cause distress by telling ourselves we have no choice. Even pleasant tasks become chores when we believe we "have to" do them out of some obligation or fear. Marshall Rosenberg (2015), in his book *Nonviolent Communication: A Language of Life,* wrote that "[w]e want to take action out of the desire to contribute to life rather than one of fear, guilt, shame, or obligation" (p.136). Make the simple change from "have to" to the phrase "choose to," adding the basic human need being met by our actions. Instead of "I have to" or "I must," we can say, "I choose to because I need," and then connect with the life-enriching need behind the action. For example, imagine something you feel forced to do right now, something you "have to" do. Now, ask yourself what need is met when you do it? Personally speaking, I dislike folding laundry. I tend to grump my way through it. When I change my thoughts to the choice and say, "I choose to fold the laundry because I value having things in order," it changes my view of the task and in some way shifts my focus from being forced to do it to seeing how it serves my needs.

- **"But" and "however"**: These words act as erasers for anything said before them. "I love that sweater but…" Nobody really hears what you said prior to these words because the "but" or "however" negates it. This negative spin can bring about defensiveness. The word "but" can bring up a bit of fight or flight. When a "but" is coming, we can generally sense it. In our heads we are saying, "the but is coming, I can feel it" and with that we brace ourselves for it. The process of bracing yourself for the word doesn't create connection, it creates fear of what is to come. Replace "Yeah, but" with "Yes, and" where possible; and when not, just start a new sentence. This can be a game changer. You can even program your email composer to auto-change your "but" into "and," so you can give your emails a more positive spin.

- **Buffer statements**: We tend to use pre-emptive statements before saying something others may not enjoy hearing. We say, "With all due respect" or "I am sorry to say," or "Don't take this the wrong way, but…" These statements put the listener into a mode of defensiveness. They are not open and waiting for your words. They are bracing for impact and possibly going into some form of fight or flight. The words "with all due respect" are rarely followed by anything that has to do with respect.

- **"At least"**: When responding to another's pain, nothing comes off as more patronizing and arrogant than the words "At least…" Imagine your house burns down, you're upset and worried. Your neighbor pops round and says, "At least you're insured." These statements can minimize a person's experience rather than empathize with it. It is a form of sympathy rather than empathy. Brené Brown (2007, p.55) writes about this in her book *I Thought It Was Just Me (but it isn't): Telling the Truth About Perfectionism, Inadequacy, and Power*. She says that this "at least response is primarily about our own discomfort" and using at least is "equivalent to shutting [someone] down," instead of being empathic and seeking to understand.

- **"In-trouble":** This term sits within the punitive system. It almost says to students that they are deserving of suffering and that suffering is coming. It offers little support. We need to move both adults and students away from this idea that they are "in-trouble" toward the idea they are "in-struggle" instead. Children and adolescents do not want disconnection with you or anybody else. When they have made mistakes, like we all have, it is important that they see us as the support system they need to deal with stress and not as a source of more stress. When we see students as struggling with issues and unsolved problems, we open the possibility that we are their support system and not the source of more toxic stress or trauma.

  This idea of moving from "in-trouble" to "in-struggle" is important for us as we move away from the idea that it's our job to control children's behavior as opposed to supporting them as they get through this thing called "life." On so many levels, it is arrogant and condescending to say that we adults are the ones who rule over children. We don't. When our young ones see us as supports rather than the "hangman," they are much more likely to be honest with us about their actions. We can support more accountability as they are not afraid of what we will do to them for the mistakes. We instead see mistakes as what they are: mistakes. We all make mistakes and we all occasionally need some help cleaning them up.

- **Sarcasm:** This is the use of irony to mock or tease, and it doesn't belong in the classroom *ever*! Sarcasm is a fun way to make your friends laugh. Some teachers use sarcasm as a strategy to connect with students. Others use it as a way of expressing their annoyance with students with a touch of humor. It goes beyond words. Sarcasm involves body language and tone that make it work (or not). Generally, we say something we don't mean with a tone and body language that display we are not serious about what we said. For the most part, a very large portion of students (especially young ones) not only don't get or understand sarcasm, they hear it as literal and experience it as painful. Their little brains are just not there yet, so they don't always get that you're joking. Younger students, around the age of 8 years, might start to get sarcasm if it is done with a tone of voice or body language they catch. There is also a good chance they won't catch it. After that, if sarcasm is done in flat tones, they might not get it at all. Around middle school or age 11 or 12, children begin to "get" sarcasm by context without the audio or tonal cues. Of course, there will be some who get it and some children who don't. Sarcasm is dependent on empathy and cognitive flexibility. For others to "get it" they have to be able to stand in your shoes. That requires relationship and it requires a student with some emotional intelligence. Children who struggle with behavioral skills may also struggle with empathy and social skills, so sarcasm might go right over their heads. Even if they do get it, we might ask if this is what we want students to learn from us (i.e., mindfulness). Sarcasm is a form of teasing and it models behavior we don't want from them, so why would we do it? Using sarcasm tells students in subtle ways that teasing others is okay. For the most part in their development, they don't have the social skills built up to understand when this is appropriate and when it is not. It needs to be removed from the school culture.

- **Mislabeling:** We also want to be careful of the words we choose as we label the behaviors we see. For far too long, we have labeled children's behavior using a vocabulary taken from the criminal justice system. The danger is that we criminalize behaviors that are responses to trauma or behaviors that are developmentally normal. For example, children who may have experienced a lack of access to food or even starvation in utero may gorge or hoard food even if they have access to it now. They may do what is considered or labeled stealing in the minds of some adults. We might even call them a "food thief." Labels like that are problematic, because using a criminal term to describe their behavior may drive us to react with a punishment. If we see that same behavior as an adaptive strategy used as protection from starvation, it might drive us to respond with supports. Another example of when we use criminal vocabulary is when we refer to minor fights in school as "assault" or "disorderly conduct." Children do occasionally fight. It is not ideal, and it is still developmentally normal. When we see two elementary school children fighting, if we label that as assault, our drive may be to punish. If we label that as aggressive behavior, we respond with lessons on anger, self-regulation, and conflict resolution. Some schools have gone as far as writing their code of conduct using the language of the criminal justice system. Minor infractions or behavior issues get labeled as class-level offenses. That vocabulary again, is borrowed from the criminal systems. These vocabulary choices have led some US schools to outsource school discipline to the courts and the police.

At the heart, using restorative language is about stepping into a student's world. Without connection, students are in their world where we judge them as "ignoring us," and we are in our world where students judge us as not caring about them. When we bring in connection, we have choices. Either we can have them step into our world and connect, or we learn to gently step into theirs and connect. Language is extremely important in this connection process. We need to use our words in ways the bring us together, focused on the long-term goals instead of short-term compliance. This is where we speak a language of support rather than judgment. Judgment shuts students down and we need to connect and build relationship with them. Our words and tone of voice need to speak to students in ways that say, "Hey, we all make mistakes. How do I support you in cleaning this one up?" Keep in mind that the voice we use when they are young becomes the voice in their head when they are older. We use restorative language when we pull students aside for a chat and stay present to them. We may use the restorative questions, or we may just use an opener of "What's up?" and then deeply listen to their answers. It involves reassuring them we are their supports and not their punisher!

NONVERBAL COMMUNICATION

We must also take note here that not all communication is verbal, and our nonverbal language also needs addressing. The hand gestures, facial expressions, and body stances we use can alter and change our messaging. To keep those things trauma-informed, we want to take a moment to be mindful that our body communicates what our words don't. We have to remember trauma impacts different children (and adults) in different ways. What sets one kid off might calm another. We need to recognize and respond to the child in front of us and that can be unpredictable. Here are a few pointers.

Height

Bring yourself down to the child's level, especially with some younger students. Towering over a child can be frightening for them. It also says something about power. Getting down to their level can be a way of showing respect for them and it also can be a way of de-escalating them.

Posture

Humans tend to read each other very quickly. Our brains tend to scan for danger on a regular basis. For those exposed to traumatic situations in their past, that scanning may increase. We want our posture to match this nonjudgmental, nonthreatening, supportive message we convey with our body. Arms wrapped around you with head down may be read as protective or lacking in confidence. A stern stance with hands crossed at chest level may be seen as a threat or a judgment. Pacing or fidgeting can be seen as nervous or worried. In this approach, the suggestion is to stand shoulder width apart with your hands loosely at your side, always below your waist.

Eye contact

It always needs to be said that culturally, eye contact has different meanings, many of which are intertwined with power, authority, and respect. Depending on culture, eye contact can be a sign of disrespect, or it can be a sign that you're listening to an adult by looking at them in the eye.

Some Eastern cultures see long periods of eye contact as a challenge to authority. Be mindful that your culture may not be the culture of your students. Some parents have told their children to look at the floor when they are being spoken to, whereas others may have demanded eye contact. Know your students and try to respect the place they come from even if it is different than yours. Eye contact or a lack of it can also be a trigger of fear. That can be overwhelming to think about since both making and avoiding eye contact with students or others who come from hard places can be triggering. It is a reminder that this whole spectrum of ideas that make up trauma-informed restorative schools is about being, not doing. This isn't so much about doing the right thing or wrong thing. It is about recognizing why, when you made eye contact and little Billy freaks out, this "might" have happened; it may help you to feel more comfortable that little Deshawn is looking at his feet when you talk to him about his outburst.

Proximity

Standing by students who struggle to behave may be seen as supportive for some and invading to others. Again, you want to watch the reactions of your students. For many students who have come from hard places, physical boundaries can be skewed. Some may put up boundaries that restrict who is near, whereas others seem to have a weak sense of boundaries. Some may invade other people's personal space, whereas others keep their distance for safety. This comes down to staying careful and monitoring student reactions. It can be frustrating that there is no simple flow chart for students with trauma, so watching reactions and monitoring their mood becomes highly important and mindful.

In Chapter 12 we will explore the use of respect agreements. This approach to creating a classroom consensus on what behavior looks like will require the five skills described in Section 2 along with our restorative language from this chapter. We want to build an agreement about respect built on a language of respect.

Respect Agreements

This chapter will focus on the creation and use of respect agreements in our school community. We are going to take a pause from the traditional ways we have created norms or class contracts to look at how stories about respect can be more impactful on behavior than just listing rules.

I was asked to observe a 7th-grade class in a local school to perhaps offer the teacher some feedback on how he could interact better with students. The teacher reported that students talked back, slept, ignored him, and in some cases they heckled him like he was a stand-up comedian telling terrible jokes. He stood at the front of the room trying his best to keep their interest in the subject, interrupting himself to bark at them, "Take off the hoodie," and "Okay, enough with the jokes," and "We need to take this seriously if you're going to pass the exam." The teacher said to me, "We have a group agreement, and everyone signed it." I looked over the nicely laminated poster hanging on the bulletin board with lots of scribbled signatures. I saw rules like "Come in and get seated with book out" and "No talking while the teacher is talking." It looked reasonable enough to me, so I asked, "Who came up with this agreement. Did the students write this?" He said, "No, I did, but they all said they agreed!"

I was talking with another teacher at a charter school. She explained her challenge of students using their cell phone during class time. She was supposed to take the cell phones away and didn't want to engage in the power-struggle to make that happen. She was also tired of writing referral after referral to the office for students using their phones. I asked her if she had developed any class norms or an agreement with her students about how they would interact with each other. She said, "No, the rules are in the school rule book. They all know what the rules are." It has been my experience that this teacher is right on the money when she says they know the rules. Students do know what is expected of them most of the time, just like we all know it is a rule in many places not to talk on your cell phone while you are driving a vehicle.

Just because students know what the rules are, there are no hard-and-fast guarantees anyone follows them. Here are three considerations: First, students usually do know the rules, or rather "what is expected of them." Second, they don't always have the skills to follow through. Third, children and youth (and adults) are skilled at justifying a reason to break the rules because they had a need to meet and lacked the choices about how to meet it.

Restorative schools are built on relationships, and relationships are built on respect. Dennis Littky, founder of Big Picture Learning and the Met School in Providence, Rhode Island, wrote something that stood out about respect in his book *The Big Picture: Education is Everyone's Business* (2004, p.55):

> When it comes to education in the United States, most people think respect is about kids calling teachers by their last names, saying "yes, sir" and not doing bad things in front of teachers or principals. To me, respect includes everyone—kids, parents, custodians—and everything. We must have and demonstrate respect for others, ourselves, and for the school building itself. *If kids are going to be respectful, they must feel respected.* And respecting them means allowing them to make decisions about the things that affect them and, most of all, believing in their potential.

In their book *Discipline That Restores: Strategies to Create Respect, Cooperation, and Responsibility in the Classroom*, Claassen and Claassen (2008) offer a new way of creating classroom norms by way of creating respect agreements. More than just creating an agreement of what is and isn't acceptable to the group, these agreements tend to force students to define respect and what it will look like for them through their lens.

Respect is a hard thing to define when one adds culture, family, age, religion, and such into the mix. More than anything, respect agreements give us an opportunity to allow communication to connect us about respect. It helps us bridge the generational, cultural, and gender gaps that can occur when we don't truly have dialogue about respect. It is important for us as a community to neutralize the power imbalances that can occur when a dominant group gets to define respect for the whole school. Respect can't be defined by one person, age group, gender, or culture. We need to learn about what respect means to the very people who will be impacted by it. It is a piece of equity in education that needs to be non-negotiable if our goal is to promote cultural humility.

The way schools currently define respect is usually dominated by the adults, even when those adults don't share the same culture, race, religion, gender, etc. of the students they teach. More simply, educators don't always look like the students they teach. We also fight the myth that respect is "earned." Respect is the default communities have with each other when they prioritize relationships. You don't earn it. Respect is what we offer each other to honor each other's humanity. It is disrespect that is earned.

In my experience as a consultant and trainer, whenever I ask a group of students how they want me to show them respect, they are like deer in headlights. I get questions like, "What do you mean?" and "Are you serious?" This is often followed by story after story of how students have experienced teachers and adults not meeting their needs for respect or who have gone far enough that students were left deeply hurt and craving respect. Eventually, students throw out ways they want to be respected and it sounds like "Don't talk down to us," or "Don't yell at us," and "Don't assume we don't know stuff, because we might." This is another reminder that we benefit most when we model respect for students by showing them respect. Listen to their opinions even when you don't want to listen or disagree. We must speak respectfully to them if we want them to speak respectfully to us.

Avoid referring to respect agreements as rules. There is benefit in calling the individual items either requests, agreements, or actions plans. Agreements made of rules, rather than requests, may sound more like demands. We don't want our students to create a document of "rules" they blindly follow out of obedience. We are creating an agreement of how we want to "be" together in community. It is best to think of this as notes from a conversation about how students and teachers want to "be" together in community. This simple language change asks students to do these things because it contributes to each other's well-being, rather than just compliance or people pleasing.

Keeping this focus on narrative and the notes of your conversations also allows students to go deep into dialogue about the agreements they make and attach them to meaningful stories. In one school where I was helping to create a respect agreement for a 6th-grade class, we were passing the talking piece around the circle and asking students to talk about why respect for our teachers was important. One girl took the talking piece and spoke of how she had started to believe teachers were not always shown respect from students. She said, "We need to treat our teachers as good as we treat our moms, because they need to go home at night and live with how we treated them." The teacher sitting next to me burst into tears. I later learned that this student and her teacher had not been having the best year together.

Another reason to emphasize that respect agreements are not a list of rules is so we can think differently about what happens when agreements are not kept. When people break the agreement, it's about the harm caused and not about the rule broken. Respect agreements can act as a working document, an ongoing conversation starter. The first question when an agreement is broken is always "What happened?" It may be time to circle up. It may be time for a restorative dialogue using the restorative questions.

A bonus of respect agreements is that when we, as adults, break the agreement we made—and we will—we get a teachable moment to model accountability. Students respect a teacher who is willing to apologize when they lose it or disrespect their students. Coming in the next day and saying, "I wasn't as respectful to you as I would have liked to have been, please accept my apology" helps to model accountability and respect for them. Even stopping mid-yelling and saying, "I am sorry. I agreed in our respect agreement that I wouldn't yell and I am." Students are much more willing to own their behavior when they see you doing it too! If we want a culture of accountability, we must hold ourselves accountable, too. Part of restorative is recognizing behavior not as something to control, but something to learn from. That includes your behavior as the adult.

HOW TO USE THE RESPECT AGREEMENT

The agreement becomes a communication tool in the classroom for when things are not going as expected. When students are not following the agreement, we pause and check-in with them to see if it needs adjustment or discussion. It is a way of checking back on the expectations we agreed to as a classroom community. We are not using it as a list of rules. We are using it as a conversation that is ongoing about what respect is and how we do it. It is an ongoing social and emotional lesson. You may not even have to bring the agreement up at all. Claassen and Claassen (2008, p.41) write:

By just walking near the respect agreement hanging on the wall I send a message to the ones who are disturbing others and themselves. They know instinctively that I am indirectly addressing them. I even get the attention of some I had not realized were drifting. The beauty of it is, often I do not even need to say anything. It talks to them for me because it invites them to talk to themselves and reminds them of what they need to be doing.

There also needs to be a word of caution about using the word "rules." That term tends to bring up some negative connotations for some students as they associate breaking rules with getting punished. In her book *Circle in the Square: Building Community and Repairing Harm in School*, Riestenberg (2012, location 1455) supports this argument when she writes:

> Many [circle] keepers prefer to use the terms "common agreements" or "guidelines" rather than the word "rules." "Rules" suggest rigidity and are found in the student handbook, which is a legal document. Rules tend to be set by authorities. In Circles, the participants generate the guidelines, which everyone agrees to follow. The spirit of "guidelines" or "common agreements" can be found in the poetic agreement suggested by one boy in a middle school Circle: "Don't step on anyone else's dream."

CREATING RESPECT AGREEMENTS

Here is the lesson plan draft for creating respect agreements:

1. In circle, after doing an opening and a mindful moment, and a check-in question, maybe an icebreaker, ask students to define respect and write down their answers. Once students have written down their own definitions, ask them to share with each other in small groups of three or as a whole group depending on the size of the class, what they have written.

   - Ask students about times where they felt respected and how to describe it.

   - What does respect look like in their families?

   - Ask students to talk about being disrespected and how that felt.

    – Ask why respect matters anyway.

    – Ask if respect is automatic, earned, or both.

2. Next ask students to fold a piece of paper into quarters. At the top of each quarter, guide students into labeling each section as follows:

    – Students respecting students.

    – Students respecting teachers.

    – Teachers respecting students.

    – Respect for the space.

3. Next, going one block at a time, look for the stories about each of these topics. You can use prompting questions, such as:

"Tell me about a time where you saw students showing each other respect."

"Tell me about a time where you saw students not showing respect for each other."

"Describe what it feels like when teachers show you respect."

"Have you ever felt a teacher showed you respect?"

"How would you like to be respected?"

"Have there been times when you don't feel you were respected by a classmate, teacher, or adult?"

"Are there times you have not shown others the respect you would have liked?"

4. Next, cultivate some agreements from the stories. Listen for the human needs, the requests, and the feelings in the stories. Our agreements will hold much better when they are based on real experiences and stories about respect.

Table 12.1: Sample Respect Agreement

Students respecting students	Students respecting teacher

• Stand up to what you think is right.
• Be kind to all—no matter what!
• Respect each other's property.
• Golden Rule: Treat others the way you want to be treated.
• If you make a mistake, own it.
• Respect bubble space.
• If you don't have anything nice to say, don't say anything at all.
	• Follow directions the first time they are given.
	• Golden rule for everyone (specials and Subs):
	  – Speak kindly and politely.
	  – Take time to listen and reflect before responding.
	  – Be flexible.
	  – Assume the best.
	  – Allow the teacher to be the leader.
	  – Be "learning ready."

Teacher respecting students	**The space**
• Don't jump to conclusions. • Check your tone (don't yell). • Choose words wisely. • Warning/explanation before a call home. • Be considerate of students' feelings. • Give students space if we aren't ready. • Don't call me out. Speak privately. • Keep track of time.	• Clean up after yourself. • Be kind to our classroom community (our stuff). • Don't destroy other people's belongings. • Take care of your own stuff. • Don't pollute the air. • If it's not yours, leave it. • Take pride in school.

Example agreements taken from K-12 classrooms in Connecticut.

VARIATIONS ON THE LESSON PLAN

- Give students some reading on respect before doing the lesson.

- Allow students to interview family members about how respect is shown in their culture.

- Do each quadrant on a separate day, always basing the theme of the day on story and narrative. Keep in mind that this is not about getting a list. It is about having a conversation.

- Add a section for guests or substitute teachers.

For substitute teachers

Check to see if a respect agreement already exists for the class. If it does, ask the students to go over it with you and see if there is anything they would like added to the "Teacher respecting students" section. This is also a space to add anything you might request of students in the "Students respecting teacher" space.

Staff respect agreements

Not long after I started sharing the idea of respect agreements with educators, I was asked to create one with a group of teachers who were struggling with workplace conflict. It had gotten so bad that one teacher was reprimanded for going into the classroom of another teacher and starting a screaming match over a borrowed stapler. No big surprise that the students in that school mirrored the conflicts of staff right back at them with behavior struggles.

Creating a staff respect agreement is not only a way of building community and setting expectations *with* youth rather than *for* them, it also is a way for adults to start a conversation about what is a respectful workplace. We sometimes forget that a trauma-informed school is also a trauma-informed workplace. Follow a similar format with staff as you would with students by putting them into circle. Create Staff to staff, Administration to staff, and Staff to administration quadrants, using the last quadrant for whatever suits the group. For example, the last quadrant could be used for meeting norms, break room care, or even agreements around the school environment.

Create the staff respect agreement in parts. Start with where the conversation is most relevant to the group. Walk toward any conflicts the staff may have, not away from them. When staff in a school are at odds with each other, it overflows onto students and the overall climate and culture of the school. Circling staff up to discuss those conflicts can be extremely powerful. When staff become a strong community of educators, they can foster a strong community of learners.

✶ ✶ ✶

Respect Agreements are an investment of time upfront with big payoffs if used consistently and compassionately. Students are going to fail to follow the agreements. Adults will fail at them as well. It isn't about following rules. It is about creating a dialogue and community. It is about building and maintaining relationships.

In Chapter 13 we explore Collaborative and Proactive Solutions, a model developed by Ross Greene that gives us new tools for preventing challenging behavior while also teaching the lagging skills a student may be missing.

— CHAPTER 13 —

Collaborative and Proactive Solutions

In the model Collaborative and Proactive Solutions (CPS) its creator, child psychologist Dr. Ross Greene, proposes the idea that misbehavior in children does not stem from poor motivation (Greene 2008) and that therefore motivational strategies are ineffective to address the needs of these children. Relying on decades of research in the neurosciences, Greene suggests that the primary contributor to challenging behavior is lagging skills. These lagging skills—falling into the general categories of executive skills, language processing and communication skills, emotion regulation skills, cognitive flexibility skills, and social skills—contribute to any variety of challenging behaviors when children are having difficulty meeting certain expectations. These "unmet expectations" are referred to as unsolved problems, and they are highly predictable. In the CPS model the primary goal of intervention is to solve those problems, collaboratively and proactively. The reason why strategies that are focused on motivation and modifying behavior often do not meet the needs of these children is that such strategies are not suited to solving problems and teaching skills.

In this chapter, we will take a closer look at Greene's model. We will explore the various elements of the model and the tools that go along with it. This chapter will not "teach" you to acquire these strategies; instead it seeks to inform you of the amazing possibilities of adding this model to your trauma-informed restorative toolbox and implementation plans. Greene emphasizes the importance of formal training in this model and that it be disseminated with fidelity. As we venture into the last section of this book on implementation, the information in this chapter will offer you enough information to see how to plan, train, and find resources to bring Greene's work to your school as a part of this whole-school change.

Greene (2014a) writes in his book *The Explosive Child: A New Approach for Understanding and Parenting Easily Frustrated, Chronically Inflexible Children* that challenging behavior occurs when the demands or expectations being placed on a child exceed their skills to respond adaptively. Let's explore some of these skills and what they might look like with students who don't have them. If we begin to see these behaviors as caused by problems to solve rather than something to control in order to get compliance, we have a better chance to cultivate discipline in children through compassion rather than control.

The skills we are talking about include problem-solving, frustration tolerance, language processing, shifting from one's original idea or solution, empathy, taking another's perspective, appreciating how one's behavior is affecting others, and resolving disagreements without conflict. When the environment demands these skills, challenging behavior becomes the means by which a child communicates that they are having difficulty responding adaptatively to those demands. For example, if a child is asked to transition from math workshop to science and they lack the skills required for handling that expectation, challenging behavior may follow. The fact that the child has difficulty meeting this expectation is highly predictable, so the problem can be identified and solved proactively.

This is much different than the conventional wisdom we hold now that states children misbehave because they aren't trying hard enough or that they lack motivation. It's a move away from thinking students misbehave to get what they want or avoid responsibility. The new philosophy, as Greene (2014b) states often, is that "kids do well if they can" (p.12).

Greene suggests that there are three ways in which adults can handle unsolved problems with children. Plan A involves the unilateral imposition of a solution. Plan B involves solving the problems collaboratively. Plan C involves setting a problem aside for now for the purpose of prioritizing. Plan A is seldom deployed except in conditions of emergent, surprising safety issues. Plan B consists of three steps: First, the Empathy step, in which the primary goal is to gather information from the child so as to understand what's making it difficult for the child to meet a given expectation. This step bears some similarity to Marshall Rosenberg's Nonviolent Communication (NVC), which involves a combination of self-empathy (or mindfulness), empathic listening, and honest expression using observation, feeling, need, and request statements.

Second, in the Define Adult Concerns step, adults are entering their concerns into consideration, especially relating to why it's important for the expectation to be met (adults' concerns are usually related to how the unsolved problem is affecting the child or other people). Third, in the Invitation, child and caregiver are collaborating on solutions that address the concerns of both parties.

Solving problems collaboratively is a dance of connection that requires all the Five Skills of Restorative discussed in Section 2 of this book. Let's look at Plan A and Plan C first, after which we will explain Plan B in greater detail.

PLAN A: AN IMPOSED SOLUTION

In this plan, adults attempt to solve a problem without a child's input, involvement, or sign-off. It is a power-over tactic. This is also the demand language we talked about in Section 1. It is the "*to*" quadrant of the Relationship Matrix from Chapter 1. Plan A is adults demanding flexibility in children while modeling inflexibility. It is also likely to bring on challenging behavior rather than reduce it. It fails to identify or teach the lagging thinking skills the child may be missing. It is different than setting or reminding students of expectations. You're not using a plan when setting or reminding students of expectations.

If adults are busy proactively and collaboratively solving problems with children, Plan A could be a rare event. Sometimes Plan A is needed, and it has its place. It is only to be done in cases of protection. Rosenberg referred to that as the "protective use of force" (Rosenberg 2015, p.185). There are times when we need to impose our will on kids to protect them and keep them safe. Our intention needs to be safety and it needs to be a last resort. When two students are about to engage in a physical altercation, separating them is Plan A and it would be appropriate. If the disagreements that cause conflict between the two students are highly predictable, then Plan A is simply a stopgap measure and is unlikely to resolve those disagreements. A note of caution about Plan A is that very often using it decreases safety as it greatly heightens the likelihood students will respond poorly.

I can't tell you just how many times I have watched Plan A play-out when adults in schools escalate situations in the classroom simply by demanding compliance from children and those children pushing back.

The more the adult demands a particular outcome, the more the student resists, which of course brings the threats of calling parents, suspensions, or other punishments. Sadly, this is most often done in the presence of other students, therefore helping to set the tone and culture of power-over in the classroom. Plan A almost always comes with a price tag and the cost is relationship.

PLAN C: PRIORITIZING

As noted above, Plan C involves setting aside a particular unsolved problem, at least for now. It is not a pass. It is prioritizing: Which problems are most important for you to solve right now and is this one of them? Sometimes, unresolved problems need to be set aside while we focus on higher-priority unsolved problems. This isn't "giving in" or placating; it is strategically choosing which problems we will be trying to solve. It is also not choosing battles. I have never liked hearing that "choose your battles" mantra when talking about children. This is not a war, and children are not the enemy.

Plan C is different from *planned ignoring*. When you ignore behavior, it is about behavior. Plan C is about setting aside the problems that are causing that behavior. For example, if Sam is having difficulty completing the word problems in math and that unsolved problem is not selected as a high priority, then that expectation would be set aside for now (until some higher-priority unsolved problems have been solved). We would likely work with Sam to determine what he would be doing during math (perhaps working on problems he actually can do) until that problem eventually becomes a priority. Plan C is not about giving in. Giving in is when you've tried to get your way and resorted to giving up as a surrender.

I was surprised one day when I went to facilitate a professional development at a middle school and heard from the teachers just how much using Plan C was helpful in classroom management. It seemed that not making a big deal out of the problems we are not working on, while focusing on the problems we *are* working on, is very consistent with differentiated instruction and personalized learning, and is preferable to placing expectations on students that they clearly can't yet meet.

PLAN B: SOLVING PROBLEMS COLLABORATIVELY AND PROACTIVELY

Plan B represents an opportunity to solve problems and reduce the challenging behaviors that are associated with those problems. It is also a chance to enhance skills, improve relationships, and enhance communication. On the Relationship Matrix, this is in the "with" quadrant or what would be referred to as "restorative." It displays high levels of support for being human while at the time maintaining high expectations. This is solving and addressing the problems that cause challenging behaviors restoratively by working to prevent them. A focus of Plan B is creating connection and partnership with a student to address unsolved problems rather than blaming, judging, or punishing behavior. It is about making sure children and adults create the kind of life-serving connection where everyone is "seen, heard, and valued" (Brown 2012, p.145).

Proactive Plan B

There are two types of Plan B: Emergency Plan B and Proactive Plan B. While Plan B can be done during an incident or event—when those involved are likely in a state of arousal—that's not the preferred timing (nor is it necessary, if caregivers have identified unsolved problems proactively). The best time to solve problems is proactively. CPS is not intended as a crisis management strategy; it is very much oriented toward crisis *prevention*.

The goal is to be prepared and able to talk with a student *before* challenging behavior occurs and when everyone is calm. Trying to address an unsolved problem when both the child and/or the adult are triggered and dysregulated isn't ideal and is likely not to work. Thus, we need to make a list of the unsolved problems. It is the mantra of Ross Greene's book *Lost at School: Why Our Kids with Behavioral Challenges are Falling through the Cracks and How We Can Help Them* that "[c]hallenging behavior occurs when the demands and expectations being placed upon a child outstrip the skills he has to respond adaptively" (Greene 2014b, p.27). The best way to create this list is to use the Assessment of Lagging Skills and Unsolved Problems (ALSUP), also created by Dr. Greene.[1] The ALSUP provides a representative list of lagging skills. These lagging skills provide caregivers

---

[1]   The ALSUP, as well as many other resources for following this model are available for free at www.livesinthebalance.org.

with their new lenses, and replace characterizations such as attention seeking, manipulation, coercion, lack of motivation, and limit testing. As you find one that you would check, it is advised to stop and then complete a list of the unsolved problems that come to mind when pondering that lagging skill. Greene reminds us not to move on to the next lagging skill until you have exhausted all the unsolved problems from each. This prevents us from cherry picking our way through the list. The end goal is a list of unsolved problems we are now ready to prioritize for solving, not a list of behaviors. As you list the unsolved problems, test them by seeing how they would sound when spoken to a child. Are they an observation of what happened or a story about what happened? Are they free of judgments? Table 13.1 provides two lagging skills examples from the ALSUP in the left column, and in the right column there are examples of unsolved problems connected to those lagging skills.

Table 13.1: Example ALSUP

Lagging skills (as listed on the ALSUP)	Unsolved problems (use observation language and be specific)
Difficulty handling transitions, shifting from one mindset or task to another	Difficulty lining up with others at the end of recess to come inside Difficulty moving to reading workshop from math
Difficulty deviating from rules, routine	Difficulty when math workshop is moved to the end of the day Difficulty when music is cancelled Difficulty when other students do not raise their hands during reading

Some guidelines offered by Greene (2014b) about creating unsolved problems on the ALSUP list include:

- Don't clump unsolved problems together. A child's reason for struggling in the transition for one class could be different than another. So, transitions aren't one clumped unsolved problem. Each incident is its own unsolved problem as it may require its own solution.

- Don't turn theory about the child ("They're just attention seeking") into unsolved problems. You'll find out what's making it hard for a child to meet a particular expectation in the Empathy step of Plan B.

- Be clear about the difference between unsolved problems and behaviors. We can't really solve the behaviors. We *can* address the unsolved problems leading to those behaviors.

Preparing ourselves for a Plan B meeting

While Greene does not talk in his model about preparation for our Plan B session, it is important for us to consider being sure we are in the right head space before we move forward. Once we have identified the problems to solve from the lagging thinking skills, we can think about meeting with this student to have a Plan B conversation. Before we do so, a suggestion would be to prepare yourself before talking with this student. This is using the skill of mindfulness. We want to be sure our intentions are centered around connection and not control, revenge, or punishment. We want to be clear with ourselves what needs of ours will be met when meeting with this student. Are there any judgments we have of this student that would get in the way of us really connecting with their concerns and offering them empathy? Can we recognize those judgments for the unmet needs in us? For example, if we think the student "doesn't really care about their work" the underlying need for us might be care. If we judge the student as a "loudmouth" or "irritating," we may need to connect with our own need for respect. It is difficult to connect to a person when we have enemy images of them filling our head. This self-preparation helps us to be fully present to the student we will be collaborating with.

We also benefit in our preparation for our Plan B meeting if we think about who from the team will be meeting with the child. The best person to lead a Plan B session is the person with whom the child has difficulty meeting expectations. If that relationship is toxic or will be unhelpful, choose another adult, whom the child trusts. The adult with whom the child has trouble meeting expectations will still need to be part of the process; they just won't be the person leading the process. As noted above, the primary goal of the Empathy step is to gather information from the child about what's making it difficult for them to meet a specific expectation. In the Define Adult Concern step, the adult is entering their concern into consideration; namely, why it's important that the expectation be met. In the Invitation step, child and adult are collaborating on a solution that addresses the concerns of both parties.

The three steps of Plan B

1. Empathy step

In this step, we are using our mindfulness skills, empathic and reflective listening skills, and questions skills to stand in the shoes of our students and learn the concerns and needs they have. You'll need to resist the idea that you already know what the student's concerns are or the theories you have about the student's behaviors. This step needs us to be present, aware, and alive to the moment in front of us without judgment. It also requires some reassurance from us that they are not "in-trouble" or about to be punished. This isn't a data hunt. It is a connection. If you make a strong connection, the data will follow.

The Empathy step begins with an Introduction. The Introduction begins with the words "I've noticed that…" and ends with the words "What's up?" In-between is the unsolved problem being discussed:

Introduction: I have noticed you've been having difficulty getting started on the reading assignment this week. What's up?

We then go into our skills of empathy (see Chapter 6) and asking questions (see Chapter 7) to drill down. We need to be able to be present to what happens in the moment from this child. That could be silence, back talk, anger, or shame. Some students may honestly not know what is making it difficult to meet the particular expectations, so "I don't know" or silence is an honest response. Staying empathic, nonjudgmental, and present will give you the best opportunity for connection; and connection will present your best opportunity to gather needed information. It also doesn't have to happen in one sitting. Different steps of Plan B can happen at different times. It doesn't all have to happen sitting at a table or desk. For some students, having this discussion while walking or while doing a puzzle on the carpet can be disarming and help to relax the child.

2. Define Adult Concerns step

During this step, we share the adult concerns or perspective on the current unsolved problem at hand. It isn't a "but," it is an "and." This can't be us saying, "Well, I heard your concerns 'but' here are mine." Replace the "but" with "and." Know that you may have to go back to the Empathy step at any point during this step.

It is important to note that some children may need reassurance that their concerns are equally important as the adult's concerns. It may be challenging to express our concerns in ways that a student understands.

Honest expression can be a helpful support in articulating those concerns. So far, the conversation might look something like this:

Adult: Hey Sam, I have noticed that you've been having difficulty getting started on the reading assignment this week. What's up?

Sam: I hate reading!

Adult: You hate reading. I'm glad you told me that. Can you tell me what about reading you hate?

Sam: It's too quiet and I hate it when it's too quiet because I can hear every little sound in the room and that distracts me.

Adult: I see. You're saying when it is quiet, the other noises stand out and you hate that?

Sam: Yeah, I can hear everybody breathing, and kicking their shoes and turning the pages. I can't just ignore them. If I hear something, I have to look to see what it is.

Adult: I can see how that would be distracting.

Sam: I like reading when nobody's around to make noise.

Adult: Ah, so you like reading by yourself?

Sam: Yeah!

Adult: Are there times you like reading and don't mind if people are there?

Sam: Sometimes, I guess if just some people are around, it's okay. I don't mind Rick. He doesn't make much noise.

Adult: So Rick is okay to read around. Are there any other things getting in your way of doing your reading?

Sam: Nah, I just don't like the quiet and the little noises I can hear when it's quiet.

Adult: [Define Adult Concerns] I hear that. Can I share with you what I am concerned about?

Sam: I guess.

Adult: I am concerned about getting all your reading assignments done on time, so you'll be up to speed for the quarter.

3. Invitation step

This is where we partner to create a plan that solves the problem in a mutually satisfactory and realistic way. This step usually starts with a summary of everyone's concerns from the first two steps and is followed by an invitation to consider potential solutions. Greene suggests offering the first opportunity to solve the problem to the student. This lets them know that their ideas matter too. If we continued our conversation with Sam to include the Invitation, it might look like this:

Adult: Sam, If I understand what we are facing today, it sounds like you don't like it when it is too quiet because it heightens the distractions when sounds pop out, and I am concerned about keeping you on-track with your reading for the quarter. I wonder if there's a way for us to do something about the distractions and still make sure you're keeping on track with your reading. Do you have any ideas?

Sam: Can we play some music during reading?

Adult: Could we do that using headphones, so you don't hear everyone else and no one else is distracted by the music?

At its heart, Plan B is based in empathy (see Figure 13.1). It isn't just an intellectual exercise. It is a human experience of understanding each other's perspective. Bringing up a child's struggles can also bring up shame. We are asking them to be vulnerable and that can be hard even for adults, let alone children. In today's world, children may be conditioned into believing adults do not have any interest in their concerns and that they will most of the time "be in-trouble," without ever being asked about their needs. That is why empathy is so important. Brown (2012, p.81) writes:

> Empathy is a strange and powerful thing. There is no script. There is no right way or wrong way to do it. It's simply listening, holding space, withholding judgment, emotionally connecting, and communicating that incredibly healing message of "You're not alone."

This is why I believe Plan B is more than intellectual gymnastics. It is about connecting with children about the very thing they struggle with and saying, "I am here for you and I will support you."

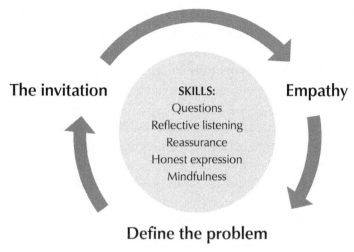

Figure 13.1: Plan B

Emergency Plan B

Emergency Plan B is when we jump into a Plan B because some "on the spot" problem-solving needs to be done. It is best if this is a rare event, however, if adults have already used the ALSUP to identify a child's unsolved problems. A couple of important points to keep in mind when dealing with anyone who is possibly in a state of fight-flight-freeze is that: 1) there isn't much oxygen-rich blood flowing to the thinking parts of the brain so reasoning with them may not be productive; 2) further trying to impose a Plan A, demand language, or adult will on the child is almost guaranteed to amp the situation up rather than calm it down; 3) telling someone to "calm down" is the last thing that will calm them down.

What is often labeled as maladaptive behavior is a human stress response. It can be adaptive. I once saw a 3rd-grade student punching the hand of an adult who was trying to pick him up and remove him from a classroom. He punched and hit the adult to try and make him let go of his arm. Later, the school wanted to suspend the student for hitting an adult. "He needs to learn he can't hit adults" was stated by more than more adult in the room. I pointed out to the group that this was most likely his brain acting in a state of fight or flight to a threat. Honestly, what human wouldn't punch and kick if a much larger person was trying to physically move them and pick them up when they didn't want to be picked up? This isn't defiance, it's a stress response.

When our stress response is activated, two main responses come into play to create what we refer to as a dysregulated nervous system. One is hyper-arousal and the other is dissociation. Hyper-arousal is the system of fight or flight that most of us are familiar with. These responses exist on a spectrum. For many students whose emotions are heightening, it is the stress response of hyper-arousal we are seeing. During this event, the brain's focus is becoming externalized where the outside threat is more a priority than internal functions like bladder function, digestion, or the headache we had. The heart rate goes up and oxygen-rich blood gets diverted from non-essential functions and sent to our muscles as we prepare to fight or flee in response to the threat. When we see the opposite in a student's response, which may look like a decrease in emotions, we may be seeing dissociation. Heart rate is decreased, and breathing may slow as they disengage from the external world. This can look like over-compliant, robotic behavior. It is why this response is often labeled by adults as "kids who don't care."

Otherwise, the process of Emergency Plan B is the same as Proactive Plan B. We're gathering information from the child in the Empathy step. We're then moving on to adult concerns. We're then considering solutions that are realistic and mutually satisfactory. Remember, Plan B works better as a prevention rather than as a crisis management tool.

Trouble-shooting our Plan B

Greene lists several missteps we can take that might derail a successful Plan B session. The first of which is that you may have fallen into Plan A. This could happen for a couple of reasons. One is intention. Greene suggests we connect with our intentions first. Did you really intend to use a Plan B, or did you come into the session with an outcome already planned? Did you come into the session genuinely valuing the student's concerns or were you caught up in your own? It is human for this to happen and it gets in the way. Intentions matter and we want to be sure we came to the session truly wanting to solve this collaboratively.

Our next reason for falling into Plan A when we are trying to do Plan B is that we got stuck with what to say. We either didn't have effective question strategies or we didn't use our empathy skills from Chapter 6. This can sometimes happen because children might not know what their own concerns are either. This can leave us feeling stumped on how to create a connection around concerns. Greene offers another reason (he calls it "Perfunctory Empathy"), which he says is the "tendency to rush the Empathy step as quickly as possible" (2014, p.118). This has a few issues, the first being the most obvious: You won't really find out the student's concerns or issues. Rushing through this step—or worse skipping it altogether—will leave you without the time to really dig into the issues. Many adults in schools are overloaded and a fast pace has become normal. Think back to our skills—this time, mindfulness. We may need to pause. While mindfulness is not explicitly a part of Greene's model, perhaps using the first few steps of P.A^2.I.R. from Chapter 5 will help us to stay present. Taking a Pause, Assessing our own intentions, Acknowledging our shared humanity, and really Inquiring about what is really happening for this student (O'Shaughnessy 2019).

Many of our students with challenging behavior have strained relationships with their peers. One way of leveling this playing field is to use Plan B with all students. We can normalize the use of this model when we are using it for all students, including doing group Plan B with the whole class. While this can seem like a monumental task, we can make this easier using the tools, practices, and skills we have learned in this book. Gathering concerns from all students in the Empathy step can be done in circle, especially when students are used to the circle process. It can useful to do this when the unsolved problems are impacting the whole group. This adds CPS to the community-building tools in our toolbox. One way of bringing a group together is to solve problems together.

As we wrap up this big picture overview of Dr. Greene's model, it is important to close on this reminder: This whole model is much like the new lens we talked about elsewhere in this book. It applies to adults as well as children. If leadership in our school is heavily relying on Plan A, then we have a "*to*" culture. When leadership stays with the thinking of Plan B, then our school culture becomes more collaborative and proactive all round. We are teaching from the "*with*" box.

✱ ✱ ✱

Our next chapter will help us understand the role of circles in restorative and how we can use them to create and heal community. We will look at the elements and stages of circle along with the various ways we can troubleshoot when they aren't going as planned. We will also look at how to design circles.

— CHAPTER 14 —

Using Circles

So far, we have explored the various ways we can set the stage for better individual relationships between community members. In this chapter, we will expand that thinking to talk about how we can use circle process to be a community. To be a community takes intentional building, maintaining, and healing. When we treat community like an eco-system that needs nurturing, we end up growing relationships that can flourish despite challenges. We build a widespread sense of resilience.

Circles are an important part of the restorative process. Circles are how members of a restorative community come together in dialogue. They may come together to build community, repair community, or rebuild it after tragedy. Circles can also be used to deliver or process academic material. Circles are a way of being together. Communities have sat together in circles for centuries. Many First Nation peoples from Africa, Australia, Canada, New Zealand, and the USA have long traditions of being in community by sitting in circle, passing a talking piece, and being humans. A quick note about language: Different countries use varying terminology for the different ways circle can be used. For the purposes of this book, a distinction is being made between a restorative or healing circle and a more formal restorative conference. There are three main types of circle:

- **Community/trust-building:** Community-building circles are used to build trust, set expectations, and allow school communities to build relationships with each other. Community-building circles need to be the foundation of circle process in the school culture. As we move to restorative or healing circles, the reminder is that you cannot restore a community you never built. These circles can be team-building exercises, community dialogue, or even relationship-building. They are also gratitude circles to celebrate each other and our accomplishments. While healing circles address harm or loss, community-building circles are the preventative use of circles. So often in schools, we see administrators running around the building putting out metaphorical fires in classrooms. Community-building circles help us to create a community that doesn't have as many fires.

- **Healing/restorative:** Healing circles are responsive circles that address harm, conflict, lack of supports, or grief. They can be spontaneous circles in response to events, or carefully planned conferences that bring specific people together to respond to an event. Those events do not necessarily mean someone has done something to cause harm. They can be healing from loss or tragedy. There are times that we need to come together as communities and support each other and these circles do just that. Healing circles can also be a way to address the healing of social issues like racism, homophobia, community violence, or classism. They may also be to address the harm caused by a person. We bring that person and those impacted by their actions together to find ways to heal, be heard, and hope to find some way of bringing justice.

I was asked to help facilitate a morning check-in circle in a 4th-grade class where students had been having issues getting along. We asked students in our circle to rate their day so far on a 1–5 scale, 1 being the worst day ever and 5 being so awesome, I could dance. We started with the 5s and asked one or two students to share why they were a 5. One student said, "I was excited to come to school today to be with my friends." Another student chimed in with "I'm a five because the sun came out and I'm sick of the rain." We went down the list of 4s and 3s who said, "Today's a 3 because I didn't want to get up this morning" and another said, "Today's a 4 because I am feeling tired." I always combine the 1s and the 2s, and one student who had been particularly quiet during all of this said, "Today is a 1 for me because my brother was arrested last night, and they took him away. I miss him." He was visibly upset. Suddenly, another student grabbed our talking piece and said, "My brother had to move to South Carolina and I really miss him. I know how it feels." One by one, other students talked about how there was someone in their life whom they missed. A few students spoke of a relative who had passed, while others talked about relatives who had been incarcerated. The empathy and support for the student feeling sad was extremely moving.

- **Academic:** Academic circles are used to discuss curriculum and learning. These can be discussions related to the material being taught or check-out circles about the things that people are struggling with or learning. Academic circles can also be used for processing content after a didactic lesson, having students engage in meaningful dialogue about the material and helping each other to give the material relevance in their lives. At one school where I was working, the 7th grade had a circle on the hero's journey, exploring "What is a hero? What is the call to adventure? Who were the mentors and helpers?" It gave students a chance to explore the curriculum while building community and social skills at the same time.

These types of circle are not mutually exclusive. A community-building circle can be healing, and an academic circle could certainly build community. Some circles could be healing, academic, and build trust and community. The goal of all circles is connection. The reason we chose to come together in circle is to connect with one another in community.

Circles in the school setting with students teach many of the thinking skills that are lagging for those with challenging behavior. The experience of using a talking piece can help students build frustration tolerance. Working together in circle addressing issues helps build their problem-solving skills. The connection and community that comes from circles also build their social skills.

THE BASIC ELEMENTS OF THE CIRCLE PROCESS
A talking piece

A talking piece is something of meaning passed from person to person to designate whose turn it is to speak. It can be just about anything, and better still something that has meaning and value to either the circle keeper or the group. Some First Nation and Native American tribes use feathers. Some New Zealand classrooms use a Māori carved talking piece. Many classrooms in the USA use a stuffed toy representing the mascot of their schools. The talking piece acts as a facilitator of the circle, helping to equalize power. Rather than a person deciding who gets to talk and about what, our talking piece does that.

Always pass the talking piece in order. Don't allow it to "pop-corn" or randomly jump to any person wishing to speak out of order. Always ask for each person to be offered a space to speak their truth by having them hold the talking piece for their time. Allowing the talking piece to go in order from person to person allows space for every voice to be heard. When we allow people to determine who gets the talking piece versus the talking piece allowing people to talk, it takes away the meaning, value, and power of the process. They can pass if they like, and if they do, they hold onto the talking piece and ask themselves three times if they would like to speak—once from their heart, once from their mind, and once from their soul. If they still want to pass, they may. You can also use the "ten-second rule." This is used as a circle guideline that asks participants who want to pass to hold the talking piece for ten seconds before passing it. This prevents students from just passing it around without thought.

At times, it may make sense to suspend the talking piece. This is preferred over having it jump around the circle. It loses its meaning when we allow people to choose who gets the talking piece to talk versus having the talking piece designate who gets to talk. If anyone just grabs the talking piece and talks, it may lose significance. If the circle requires some discussion, you can suspend the talking piece for a while. When the discussion is concluding, it may benefit the circle to return to having the talking piece continue in rounds.

Nikita's collar

I always suggest to people that the talking piece needs to be something with meaning. Grabbing a rubber ball might work and yet it is nowhere near as good as something with meaning.

While I have several talking pieces I use, my favorite is my late dog Nikita's collar. She was a rescue dog adopted from a shelter. When I first decided to adopt a dog, I wanted a dog to pick me rather than me picking a dog. I didn't know how I would know. I just knew that I would know when this dog chose me. When I met

Nikita, she was in her cement-block kennel and she pressed her whole body against the fencing to be closer to me while I rubbed her head. The shelter representative mentioned they had another dog of the same breed in the other part of the shelter. When I stood and began to walk away from Nikita, she began to whimper and cry. I knew then that she was asking me to adopt her and I did.

Nikita became my lesson in being trauma informed. She, as it turned out, had been badly abused and mistreated. She was seriously underweight and her fur was thinning. When I would raise my hand just to scratch my head, she would squat down, shaking, with her little ears down, tail down, and her bladder would let go. My partner asked me if I wanted to take her back to the shelter and hence my first lesson in working with trauma was don't give up.

Then came my second lesson—to love relentlessly. Persistence prevailed and with lots of love, patience, and the ripping up of all carpets in the house, we managed to break her fear and allow her to feel safe with us. It took changing how we reacted to her fear. It also took some adjustments to our lives and, most importantly, we never gave up on her. She spent the next ten years of her life being the happiest dog one could imagine.

One of the big things that helped our dog and us was involving a canine behaviorist. I remember our first appointment. She took Nikita and placed her in the kennel with the other dogs to play. I got a little confused and said, "I thought you were going to train our dog?" She giggled a bit at this and exclaimed that she "doesn't train dogs, she trains owners." That was my third lesson—when you don't know what you are doing, find someone who does.

Sadly, Nikita developed brain cancer and I had to send her over the rainbow-bridge. Looking back on the things she taught me, I realize she taught me to rethink trauma. She helped me understand triggers and how her fear system responded to triggers. Mostly, she taught me about resilience. She taught me that we can go through some rough stuff and still remain loving. She taught me that we can go through trauma and come out stronger on the other side.

I use her collar as a talking piece and tell this story. I want people to think about resilience when they hold it. I want them to think about the strength that one can muster up when given safety and love.

> I am amazed at the number of people who comment to me how
> much they were touched in the circle by Nikita's collar.
>
> I remind people of the three big lessons: 1) Don't give up; 2)
> Love relentlessly; 3) When you don't know what you're doing, find
> someone who does.

A circle keeper/facilitator

This is a person who is responsible for facilitating the circle while also being a participating community member. They are not "in-charge" of the circle as much as they are the person charged with keeping the space. Circle keepers are not tasked with "fixing" or "managing" the circle. Circle keepers do need to model the skills of restorative (e.g., mindfulness, asking questions, empathic listening, and honest expression). A circle keeper asks questions, holds participants to agreements, and, unlike a mediator, acts as both participant and keeper. The keeper does not direct the content of the group, only the process. A keeper is often responsible for making sure a talking piece is available. Circle keepers may be asked to choose a location for a circle, craft the questions that will be asked, choose a topic of discussion, and write any follow-up plans or agreements that are reached in the circle.

A round

A round is when the talking piece has made its way around the full circle.

Circle guidelines/agreements

Each group will want their own agreements of how they will be together in community. It is best when those agreements are made by consensus. Consensus as a process asks us to agree, stand aside, or block a decision. This is unlike our common way of gaining group approval, which generally has relied on majority rule. Here we want agreements to be made with the consideration of all, even when some voices dissent. We may need to devote a circle just to having common understanding of the guidelines we choose. Here are some possible agreements or guidelines groups may decide to adopt:

- **Confidentiality (respecting privacy):** Each circle group will want their own agreement around what can be shared with others, especially when talking about ongoing circle groups such as advisory or morning circle. This subject always stirs up the concerns from staff about mandatory reporting laws. It is important that students are aware about mandatory reporting and our obligations as educators to those rules. Students can and do use the safety of the circle to share sensitive and sometimes revealing information about their lives. It may also be the time they choose to ask for our support and help. Circles are not the most appropriate place for students to reveal abuse. Circle keepers may want to choose to stop students or others from disclosing that information if we think it is happening.

- **Respect the talking piece:** A circle keeper may choose to add some weight to the meaning of the talking piece by asking for agreement from the participants to hold the talking piece in a place of honor and respect.

- **Speaking and listening from the heart:** Using the talking piece as a guide, participants are asked to speak only when they are holding the talking piece. They are invited to speak from their truth vulnerably when they are holding the talking piece and to listen in a way that allows others to be vulnerable.

- **Saying as much as is needed and no more:** Having agreements that participants will be mindful of time and respect for each other, agreeing that they will say only what they need to and no more, allows a chance for everyone to share and speak from their heart. It is asking each person to be considerate of others without feeling rushed. This agreement helps to teach valuable social skills.

Centerpiece

Some US-based and Canadian circle keepers use a centerpiece for the circle. This is generally influenced by Native American or First Nation traditions. This can be a candle, a colorful fabric, or even a collection of meaningful objects to the participants. For restorative circles, participants can be asked to bring meaningful objects for the centerpiece. It symbolizes that here in the circle there are no sides. We are here to focus our energy on the center of healing and community. It needs to be noted that using a centerpiece without acknowledging where the tradition comes from and using those traditions without respect of their origins can cross the line of cultural appropriation. Ask students if there are special items they would like added to the center. The centerpiece also brings an element of ritual into circle. Giving students a sense of ritual helps to build resilience. It lifts the practice of circle, allowing students to feel they are part of something that will be there for them when they need to bounce back from adversity.

Opening/closing

Making sure the circle has a distinct and unifying opening and closing that marks where it begins and ends helps participants of the circle to hold the space and time as different than a regular meeting. It is a way of saying to one another, "We are in circle," and that means something. Openings and closings can be as simple as a quote, a reading, or even a short breathing meditation.

STAGES/STRUCTURE OF A CIRCLE

Boyes-Watson and Pranis (2015), in their book *Circle Forward: Building a Restorative School Community*, offer some possible stages of the circle. The stages are an outline of what actions will be taken during a circle. Follestad and Wroldsen (2019) also offer some possible stages or what they call the "structure" of circle in their book *Using Restorative Circles in Schools: How to Build Strong Learning Communities and Foster Student Wellbeing*. Here are some possible stages that could be used to design a circle:

- **Welcome:** Take the time to greet everyone and bring them into the circle. This is the time for any announcements that need to be made or logistics that need to be mentioned.

- **Mindful moment:** Sometimes just asking people to breathe for a minute (or two) is a great way to center and calm everyone in the room. This could also be a time for a mindfulness activity.

- **Opening/unifying starter:** The opening can be a quote, a short reading, a poem, or even a song to set the tone of the circle and to signal when the circle begins.

- **Purpose:** This can be done as part of the welcome or as a separate piece. It gives people a vision for what the circle will address. For example, a circle on friendship, respect, or listening.

- **Check-in round/check-out round:** A check-in round and a check-out round (see below) are important. This is a way of gauging where circle participants are in their emotional space. Some popular ways of doing these check-in or check-out rounds is to either use comparison questions ("If your day was like the weather, a color, a song, what would it be?") or sentence competition ("If you really knew me, you would know...").

- **Ice-breaker:** This is a fun way to get students feeling comfortable in circle and can also be a way to build community. The idea is to play short games or do activities designed to help participants get to know each other better or even work better together.

- **Values:** Some circle keepers may decide to explore the group's values and even use those to inform making circle guidelines.

- **Agreements (guidelines):** A reminder of the group agreements made for participants to be able to work well together.

- **Storytelling:** Especially in harm circles, it is important that each person is afforded the opportunity to tell their story from their perspective. Often for those impacted by harm this is the chance to feel a sense of comfort in being heard talking about their experience and pain. For those who have created harm, it is a chance to explain, to understand the impact on others, and to seek atonement. In community-building circles, this may be a time to share experiences related to the theme of the circle.

- **Restorative questions:** During a harm or restorative circle, this may be a time to use the restorative questions to explore the story and the harm, reserving the questions about repair of that harm until the next step where topics are explored.

- **Exploration of topics:** This may be the time when a circle keeper uses prompting questions to explore topics and deepen everyone's understanding of those topics. For example, if a theme of the circle appears to be justice, the circle keeper/facilitator may want to ask a prompting question about what justice means to each person.

- **Check-out round:** As the circle nears its close, this may give participants a place to park any lingering thoughts on what has occurred in the circle. Participants may use one word or a sentence about how they are leaving or what they experienced in the circle.

- **Closing/unifying closer:** Much like the opening, this can be a short quote, or even an exercise, a moment of silent mindfulness, to signal the end of the circle. This can be powerful as so many circles have emotional moments and it may be a way of offering closure to those moments rather than leaving them hanging. This may be the time you ceremoniously extinguish the candle you lit or even ring a chime to signal the end or close of the circle.

- **Thanks:** Depending on the closing you choose, it may be appropriate to thank people for coming and then end the circle. My personal experience is that this is better to just use the words "Thank you" and then stand to signify the circle time has ended.

PLANNING FOR A CIRCLE

There are many considerations when planning a circle. For our continuing, pro-social and community-building circles, these plans are more ongoing and require less time to develop. They can also be reused. They involve simple things like deciding the theme of the circle, what prompting questions to use, and who will be the circle keeper. Having students involved in the keeping of circles and the planning process for them can be a great skill-building tool.

Setting up the circle

While asking students to move furniture around and clearing space for circle can sound cumbersome, once students get into a habit or ritual of setting up for circle, it can become pretty routine. Some students can have the "job" of setting up the centerpiece if you are using one. It is best to set up a circle of chairs without any obstruction in the middle. While for younger students, a circle on the carpet can work, just be sure the circle keeper sits on the carpet as well.

Planning for a healing circle

When responding to harm in our communities by using a circle, we want to take great care to ensure the circle is focused on repairing harm without creating more harm. We do not want to create a situation where those who feel victimized end up becoming further traumatized. It is important to consider a few key precautions:

1. **Choosing the participants:** Making sure you have the right people in the circle is important. Ensure that those who have created harm and those impacted by that harm have a voice in the circle. Finding out who the key stakeholders are in the incident is important to having an outcome that meets the needs of all involved. Those involved in an issue know the issue best.

2. **Pre-circle meetings:** Have the circle keeper or Restorative Justice coordinator speak with each person who will be involved with the circle to explain the process, ask what they are hoping to get out of the circle, and perhaps coach them on telling their stories. This pre-circle meeting provides a chance to be sure each person comes to the circle fully understanding that this is an alternative approach and not a punishment session. It offers a chance to explain the restorative questions or other circle elements that may be followed. It also builds trust with the circle keeper, which can offer some students and participants a sense of safety. It is in the pre-circle meeting that we may determine a participant is not ready for the circle at this time. It isn't wise and can even be dangerous to bring people into the circle who are not willing or ready to be there.

3. **Assessing accountability:** If we are doing a healing circle that involves a student or students who have created harm, the circle will be focused on the full picture of the incident. Doing a circle or any restorative process where a student is only taking minimal responsibility for their actions or where they take no responsibility for their actions is tricky. A student who is unwilling to be accountable or explain themselves may still benefit from a circle. They may benefit from processing the impact of their actions on those they have harmed by hearing the impact of their actions through the stories of those affected. It may seem disappointing to others in the circle when they don't take the accountability we

are requesting to repair the harm. It leaves us with a choice to have or not have the circle. Having the circle may provide them with an opportunity to finally acknowledge their accountability after hearing from those they have harmed. They may not take the opportunity and that is a risk for everyone. Managing the risk is important. If those who have been harmed will be further harmed, do not take that risk. In seeing behavior through a trauma-informed lens, we want to avoid holding children accountable for behaviors that are survival or coping behaviors. Imagine holding a student "accountable" for fighting when they are standing up for themselves to a fellow student who was victimizing them. Imagine holding a circle for a student who stole a candy bar from their teacher only to learn that student hasn't eaten anything since yesterday. We want to be sure our restorative practices heal and do not further traumatize already struggling students.

4. **Space:** It is also important to think about space. Physically putting chairs into a circle without tables or other barriers is vital to creating connection. While desks in a circle are not terrible, they are not ideal either. It is helpful to make sure the space is one that will not be interrupted and will offer some privacy. This assures the participants some sense of confidentiality about their stories.

PHASES OF A HARM-, CONFLICT-, OR INCIDENT-FOCUSED CIRCLE

Depending on what country you are in or who trained you, there may be different terminology to describe harm circles. Some may call them conferences, restorative circles, or repair circles. For this book, a harm circle is a circle that addresses the need for healing. It doesn't need to have a responsible party, as in some cases such a person doesn't exist. Harm circles can address conflict, or even tragedies that may arise (e.g., the death of a teacher or fellow student). We do best to realize that no restorative practices use a step-by-step approach as this work isn't about doing, it is about being. Circle is a place where emotions, thoughts, and questions can be expressed freely. It is not focused on the wrongdoer; instead, attention is given to healing all who are impacted by the events or conditions that caused harm.

A conference is a similar process to a circle and is typically held in circle. It may or may not have a talking piece. Rather than a talking piece deciding who will talk and in what order, a facilitator has pre-circled with the stakeholders involved and determined who needs to speak first. Often, a primary person who has been harmed may want to speak and tell their story first. In other cases, that same person may choose to hear from the student or students who are responsible for that harm first.

Phase I: Before the circle

Using our skills of mindfulness, circle keepers need to check in with themselves to be sure the topic and participants who will be in the circle have no blocks in the way. Is there anything about this circle or its circumstances that would block you from being present and compassionate?

Phase II: Inviting participants

Either via phone or in person, contact each person invited to the circle. Take the time to explain the circle and its purpose to them. Take the time to listen to them and allow them to choose this process as a way of addressing the harm. Ask each participant if they believe there are others who are impacted by the harm whom we might choose to invite, and if so, gather any necessary contact information. It is strongly advised that each person in the circle has a support person with them who can see them in a different way than the circle sees them in this incident. A youth who is responsible for creating harm may want a supporter who knows them beyond the incident of harm. A victim of harm may want someone who can bear witness to the impact the incident has had on them. During this phase, circle keepers might want to stay present and aware of any participants who might want to use the circle for harm or revenge. It is not advised that anyone who is not yet ready to be in circle comes to circle. People must be ready and willing to be in the circle. If people do not seem ready, they may need more coaching, empathy, or perhaps they have unanswered questions. Staying present to where they are in the moment is the best method of approach.

Phase III: Prior to the circle

The purpose of the pre-circle meeting is making sure everyone understands how the circle will go and allow them to predict and expect certain aspects of the circle. They need to trust you and the process, and they need to be assured that they or their loved one will not be harmed again. It is essential to introduce participants to the restorative questions in the pre-circle conversations, asking the following questions:[1]

"What happened?"

"What were you thinking at the time of the event (or when you heard about this event)?"

"What have you been thinking about since?"

"Who has been impacted and how?"

"What's been the hardest thing for you?"

"How do you think this situation could be dealt with?"

"Who needs to be a part of the circle process?"

"How can I support you?"

It may be important to ask those impacted if there are particular needs they have, as they come into the circle. Are there things that would make things right in their eyes? This could include financial losses repaid, apologies, or other ways of repairing harm that they would like to request.

Always remember that some people may not be ready to circle. They may consider it later. They may need more trust in the circle keeper or the process. They may also just need time. Don't push people or try to "talk them into it" as it may just backfire.

This would also be the place to talk about confidentiality and mandatory reporting. Everyone in the circle needs to know that unreported child abuse, elder abuse, and threats of harm to self or others must be reported to the proper authorities.

---

1 A complete list of restorative questions can be found in Chapter 8.

Phase IV: During the circle

Once it has been established that all participants are ready and willing to voluntarily proceed, schedule a circle. The outline or agenda for a harm circle looks much like any other circle. In doing a harm circle, the talking piece may go around the circle in response to the restorative questions. It can be useful to break the rounds up into a storytelling round, a round about the impacts, and another round that addresses repairing the harm. This is the time to use the action plans we discussed in Chapter 9.

Phase V: Follow-up (if needed)

It may be helpful to bring people back together after an agreed period of time to follow-up on any action plans or agreements that were made during the circle. The group can determine who needs to be part of the follow-up circle. Again, this is best done as a voluntary action.

FACILITATING A HARM CIRCLE

When your prep work has been completed and your circle has been scheduled, it will be time to hold the circle. As participants come into the space, invite them to sit where they feel comfortable. As you welcome them to circle, take care of any logistical announcements and a welcome. It is nice to start with a unifying quote, song, reading, or other tradition. Follow that with a moment of mindfulness to allow people to arrive and settle. Next, pass the talking piece in the first round to start with a check-in so you know how people are showing up.

Sometimes, just acknowledging each person's emotional state is helpful to the circle. It allows everyone an opportunity to empathize with where others may be. To kick off the substance of the circle, after acknowledging why everyone is gathered in circle, ask the first batch of restorative questions ("What happened?" "What were you thinking at the time?" "What have you been thinking since?"). Allow each person their time to answer. Then move to the second round, asking the next batch of questions ("Who has been impacted and how?" "Has this impacted your family or friends?" "What has been the hardest thing for you?"). Again, allow each person their opportunity to answer. The final round may be to ask what happens next. If this is a circle in response to an incident, it may be helpful to ask what needs to happen to make things right. It can also be helpful to ask what participants are willing to commit to. If this circle has convened in response to a tragedy, it may be helpful to ask, "What would you need to feel supported?" "What would you ask of your community?" This is where plans for healing can be made.

You may find it helpful to have a flipchart or whiteboard to write down ideas so the group can see them. It may also be necessary to create an action plan, as we discussed in Chapter 9. Facilitating harm circles takes patience and training. It is highly recommended that you only facilitate a harm circle after attending at least a basic circle training with an experienced trainer.

USING ACADEMIC-FOCUSED CIRCLES

While academic circles can follow the same format as any other circle, they can be used to process content, deliver content, and even do a harvesting of learning. For example, a circle at the end of the lesson could ask the following questions: "What was your biggest take-home from this lesson?" "What was a concept you struggled with?" "What was your favorite part of today's lesson?"

GRATITUDE AND CELEBRATION CIRCLES

Circles of appreciation or gratitude are a great way of building community and connecting people. Gratitude is a powerful community builder. There are various ways to use this tool in the restorative toolbox. You can have students share appreciation of, and gratitude toward, each other. You can have students share celebrations of their learning. You could also have students draw each other's names from a basket or paper bag and celebrate each other or the things they appreciate about each other. You could have them celebrate each other's best moments of the week or best moments of the semester.

FACILITATING A FORMAL CONFERENCE

A formal conference is used when the harm we are addressing is more serious or egregious. While the terminology may vary from country to country, typically the conference does not use a talking piece, and participants may speak in a pre-determined order based on who the victims would like to hear from first or if they would like to speak first themselves. Formal conferences may also include community partners, law enforcement, family members, or others. The impact of these circles can be deep. Conferences of this nature also require intense preparation. Examples of things requiring formal conferences might be assaults, racial incidents, fights, or even vandalism. Like healing circles, these require additional training and it is recommended such circles are facilitated by individuals with that training. Don't be afraid to use community partners to come in and coordinate these conferences if your school lacks the readiness to do it alone.

TROUBLESHOOTING CIRCLE

There is never a guarantee our circles will go the way we expect. Sometimes no one will talk; at other times no one will stop talking! Students may share more deeply than you appreciate, or they may share views you don't share. Holding space for those events can be difficult. In the following table, I have added some ideas for troubleshooting your circle.

Table 14.1: Troubleshooting the circle

If you experience this...	Try this...
Circles are taking too long	• Use a timer for each person. • Ask for one-word or one-sentence answers. Be sure to model it! • Ask the students for suggestions and solve the issue collaboratively.
No one is talking, or more students are passing than talking	• Use alternative methods of expression, such as drawing, freestyle poetry, journaling, movement, activities with no words. • Try smaller circles within the larger circle for some fun exercises. • Ask questions students are more likely to want to answer, such as "What is it you want adults to understand about youth?" • Use a partner-share icebreaker or concentric circles so every student can have a chance to talk without having to speak to the whole class. • Hold the circle in another language if appropriate. • Use less personalized circle prompting questions.

cont.

If you experience this...	Try this...
Specific behaviors are derailing the circle	• Revisit the shared guidelines and values you created together (repeating these can be very effective). • Refer to the class respect agreement (this, too, may be repeated). • Letting go of minor silliness can be useful. Students sometimes act silly because the topic or situation makes them nervous. Not giving attention to the silliness can allow it to pass. • Try to determine underlying feelings and needs that are likely being expressed through the misbehavior, and focus on those rather than the behavior itself. • Pause the circle activity and wait for students to settle. • Use activities that require students to change seats. This may help break up disruptive groups. • Engage the students who are misbehaving as circle-keepers or ask them to help plan the questions for the next circle. • Have one-to-one restorative conversations at another time with the students who are misbehaving to get to the root of the issue. • If Collaborative and Proactive Solutions have been implemented, use Plan B. • Check-in with the implementation team for feedback or coaching.
One or a few students do all the talking...	• Have students make or bring their own talking piece that is meaningful to them or their culture and ask them to speak about it in circle. • Consider giving the "natural leaders" jobs such as being a circle keeper or making a centerpiece for the circle. • In private conversations with the quieter students, ask if there is anything they need to feel safe in order to participate more fully.

Adapted from Oakland Unified School District (n.d.) Restorative Justice Implementation Guide: A Whole School Approach (pp. 25–26)

✳ ✳ ✳

Chapter 15 will focus on creating de-escalation spaces within our classrooms and schools. It will help readers set up a space where students with both sensory craving issues and sensory blocking issues can be addressed. It will also explain the various ways to use the space, and how to prevent it from being misused.

— CHAPTER 15 —

Regulation Spaces

Zen corner, recovery room, sensory room, peace room, mindfulness room, comfort corner, re-direction center, calm-down corner, time-in space, and quiet corner are all names for regulation spaces. These are spaces where students can go when they feel dysregulated or are worried that they may become dysregulated. These can also be spaces where students can go, either to get, or get away from, sensory information that may be missing or overwhelming their brain. This chapter will walk you through the ideas of having and using a space in your school or classroom where students can go to regulate their being. We will look at how to set it up, what it needs to include, and how to use it. We also want to be mindful of the ways it could be misused so that we can avoid that.

Figure 15.1: De-escalation space

Because exposure to early childhood trauma can impact each child differently, there will likely be a need for a variety of strategies. Some students may crave sensory input whereas others are trying to dull or block sensory input, so they can become regulated. Having space where students can go to decompress in rough moments is a way of preventing meltdowns and behavioral challenges and helps to teach self-regulation and self-care.

It is important to always note that often children who have experienced traumatic situations or events may have developed skills and behaviors that help support them when they are dysregulated. At the time students developed the behaviors, which may have been during or right after exposure to trauma, these skills and coping mechanisms were life-serving if not life-saving for them. While those same behaviors may no longer be serving them, this does not mean the child has the skills yet to do something different. As they learn new skills and new ways of being in the world, they may need some supports in learning to self-regulate.

According to Sorrels (2015), self-regulation has five main domains: physical, cognitive, emotional, social, and prosocial. Our ability to regulate our bodies is *physiological regulation*. We have all met the squiggly, wiggly kindergarten students and they tend to be what we think of first when we look at self-regulating our physical state. It goes further than that. It includes regulating our bodies in response to the sensory input coming into our senses as well as the sensory input coming directly from our bodies like our equilibrium (i.e., the vestibular system), our inner sensations of hunger or need to use the bathroom (i.e., the interoceptive system), or the sensations of how we move our bodies in response to our environment (i.e., the proprioceptive system). The next domain is *cognitive regulation*, which is our ability to control and purposefully use our minds. It is our ability to hold stuff in our head until we can do something with it. It also includes our ability to block out distractions and focus on a task or thought. Of course, what we seem to focus on most when talking about self-regulation is *emotional regulation*. This includes our ability to control and manage unpleasant or overwhelming emotions or feel and enjoy the pleasant ones. When children lack the ability to manage or regulate strong emotions using strategies such as words, art, music, or hand gestures, they may ultimately express those emotions through challenging behaviors. A lack of emotional regulation may also impede a child's ability to concentrate on schoolwork or make friends. Trauma can greatly impact the development of this skill. For some children, the ability to control their emotions may be stunted by their experiences of trauma. Others have been forced to develop this skill as a survival strategy. Lastly, we have social and pro-social regulation, which is how we interact and regulate ourselves in relation to other people. *Social regulation* is a child's ability to change or adapt their own behaviors, based on how that behavior impacts on others. It involves the social skills of empathy, reading facial cues, voice tones, and other messages they receive from their peers that give them vital information about their relationships. Some children exposed to traumatic events or situations may misread these social cues or lack the ability to change their behaviors in response to these cues. *Pro-social regulation* is a child's capacity to empathize and then act on that information. While it involves many of the same skills as social regulation (e.g., reading facial cues or body language), it also involves a child's ability to act or respond in caring ways to a friend's distress or in positive ways to a friend's excitement.

Trauma can greatly impact the development of any of the domains of self-regulation. In some cases, children have heightened abilities of regulation as that has served to save them; for example, the ability to walk about their house being super quiet and unheard so they don't encounter an abuser. In other cases, abuse, neglect, fetal alcohol syndrome, and other childhood traumatic events can interrupt the development of these abilities. Having a regulation space either in the school building or in a corner in the classroom may provide them with a chance to develop these skills.

A regulation space is best when it allows students to find a sense that they are safe and in control. It can be filled with tools for regulation such as coloring books or Mp3 players that contain guided meditations. It needs to be set up in a way that students feel a sense of refuge when in the space. Here are some guidelines about using the space:

- Never use it as a reward or punishment, consequence, or time-out space. Regulation space is better used as a "time-in" rather than "time-out."

- It is meant to prevent behavioral issues, not respond to them.

- Take time to introduce it to students as a positive choice so we can limit or avoid feelings of shame when using the space.

- Create some privacy for students in the space without having them feel excluded. Shower curtains or privacy screens can be helpful to accomplish this.

- Structure and time limits are helpful to prevent student misuse of the regulation space. Using an hourglass timer can be helpful for being fair with the time. Set the timer for the limit and then check-in when the timer goes off. If the child needs a few more minutes, set the timer again for less time than the first.

- Using reflection worksheets with the restorative questions or other types of reflective questions that allow students to identify and regulate their feelings can also be helpful and take them out of their downstairs brains (limbic + brainstem) and move them to the upstairs brain (pre-frontal cortex).

When creating the space, it will be helpful to include any number of different tools to assist calming and self-regulation. These may include such options as:

- soft lighting

- comfortable chairs

- earmuffs

- glitter jar

- books

- weighted blankets

- noise-canceling headphones

- sunglasses

- coloring books with colored pencils or crayons

- Mp3 players with guided meditations, soothing music, or nature sounds

- fish tank

- putty, clay, or play-doh

- massage chair covers

- sound machine

- puzzles

- pillows

- bean bags

- stress balls

- posters with positive messages

- emoji handouts or posters to help identify feelings.

In one school where I was consulting, we had a 7th grader I will refer to as Blake. He had multiple self-regulation issues for his age and struggled with making friends. Sadly, this lack of self-regulation also became the negative self-talk that reinforced his own negative beliefs about himself. To help him in his struggle when he got upset, he often went to the sensory room to calm and regulate himself. We had filled a mini-Mp3 player with some guided meditations for him to use. At first, we would hand him the player and he would just walk off holding it. Later, we observed him trying to find a way to do what he wanted with it. When that failed and he discovered no games could be played and no other music could be found, we saw him listening to the guided meditations. Within a week, he was coming to us and asking for the Mp3 player and then going into the sensory room to chill. He was timed for how long he spent in the sensory room and was sent back to class when he was feeling ready to learn. While this was no panacea for the spectrum of the trauma he was struggling with, it was clearly making a difference for him.

What many of our students need more than punishment are the skills to regulate their systems so they don't manifest as difficult behaviors. While punishments and rewards can lead to a child eventually learning the skills of regulation, they will have learned them through fear or manipulation rather than compassion. De-escalation spaces or sensory corners are a compassionate way to teach self-regulation.

✶ ✶ ✶

We have now concluded Section 3 on what restorative looks like in practice. It would be impossible for one book to cover all the amazing restorative practices that are out there. It is also impossible to cover every nuance of the practices we did cover. The best move to make now is to keep deepening our journey into the practices, always keeping in mind that this is more about *being* than *doing*. In Section 4, we will look at what it takes to implement this work on a whole-school or district level.

— SECTION 4 —

IMPLEMENTATION

CHAPTER 16

Implementation

The goal of this chapter is to help you think about the infrastructure, change management, planning, and training that needs to happen in your school or district to make implementing this work successful. At this point, there is no need to re-invent the wheel, as dozens of schools across the globe are embracing this work. We can learn from their successes and mistakes. We can also learn from implementation science the most effective ways change happens and use those lessons in our own efforts to implement change.

THE POWER OF OUR STORIES: THE IMPORTANCE OF NARRATIVE

A huge piece of this restorative work is vision, identity, and story. Narrative is an important component of the culture of any organization. It is the story we tell ourselves about who we are and what is important to us. It is filling in the rest of the statement "We are the type of school that…"

An example of such a narrative is a Connecticut high school where the faculty and staff had an array of stories about themselves as a school: "We are the school where teachers don't get along," or "People don't care about each other here," or "There is no respect." During a professional development session, they talked about the stories they told themselves about each other and themselves. As they began to recognize the stories they told themselves about themselves, they also began changing the story. Instead of "We can't get along," they changed it to "We are working toward getting along."

Stories are everywhere in our schools and communities. Some of those stories are true and others reflect our judgments, fears, or frustrations. Changing a school climate means getting a grip on the story and sometimes telling a new story. What kind of school will this be? What is the story we will tell ourselves about ourselves?

Dennis Littky, founder and principal at the Met School in Providence, Rhode Island, writes in his book *Big Picture Learning: Why Education Is Everyone's Business* (2004, p.60):

> I am a storyteller, and when I start a school, I look for the stories that will help build the culture. Like any culture with a strong oral tradition, a school culture can thrive and grow on its own stories—stories of what has been and stories of what could be.

Listen in your school, in your family, and at your workplace to the stories. What are the stories? They can be things we say that empower us or stories of our learned helplessness: "Things will never change around here" or "You can bring in this touchy-feely stuff, but we're still gonna have to suspend." These are just stories. Not only can we change our stories to empower us, we can re-write the endings of the stories we tell, if only we are ready to tell a new story.

Many schools across Australia, Canada, Europe, New Zealand, Southeast Asia, the UK, and the USA have implemented restorative approaches. Some are making huge advances and others are making lots of mistakes from which we can all learn what not to do. Some of the biggest successes in the USA have come from Oakland (California), Baltimore (Maryland), and Denver (Colorado). Many school districts in these states have offered detailed reports of what worked and what didn't. We can learn a lot from where things worked and what schools need to do to make this happen.

MY JOURNEY INTO TRAUMA-INFORMED RESTORATIVE JUSTICE IN SCHOOLS

In 2015 I was contacted by one of the largest school districts in Connecticut that had chosen five schools as a pilot. Schools needed to apply to be part of a cohort whose ten-member implementation teams would send just five members to get six full days of intensive training in Restorative Justice, trauma-informed schools, equity, and change management. As I developed the curriculum for the training, I became more and more excited about just how epic this could be. I knew other people were combining restorative and Nonviolent Communication. I just had not seen anyone combine restorative, Nonviolent Communication, mindfulness, Collaborative and Proactive Solutions, trauma work, and equity into one implementation.

We started by having an information session, and any school that planned to apply was required to attend. The information session provided a clear view of what would be expected and what data they needed to collect, and also provided support about how to form their teams. Information session participants were provided with an overview of the five skills, the expanded continuum of restorative approaches and practices, and were told stories of success from other schools where restorative practices were already in place. While a dozen schools applied, six were chosen that would be part of our first run of this change in the district. We planned the six-day training, leaving a few weeks in-between trainings, which were provided in two-day blocks. We invited the schools to send five members of their team to the training and required at least one person from each team to be an administrator as administrators are key to making systemic changes and they need a background of restorative to make these changes happen. We also required each team to have a parent voice even if that parent did not attend the training. We wanted parent voices in the planning process of each school. I also suggested that schools, where appropriate, included student voices in every way possible.

We were blessed with our first group of 30 people, including principals, teachers, behavior specialists, social workers, guidance counselors, and paraprofessionals, who came to spend six days of their lives on the journey of exploring what became the content of this book. We asked each team to begin developing a three-year change plan of how they would roll out restorative at their school. On a personal note, it was a wonderful journey for me as I had yet to spend six days teaching this material in such depth and to an audience so eager to wrap their heads around this even when they disagreed with me. The other reason this kick-off went so smoothly was down to the team on the district level that made the training happen, handled the logistics, and made sure we had resource books, food and, most importantly, coffee. Each participant was given a then incomplete draft of this book, a copy of *Circle Forward: Building a Restorative School Community* (Boyes-Watson and Pranis 2015), and access to a Dropbox folder filled with additional resources. In addition to all of the above, we provided each team with two half days of technical assistance to be used in any way that would support them. The teams could use the technical assistance time to have the trainer model circles in classrooms, modeling the creation of respect agreements, and receive additional training, or even help developing their change management plan. Some used this time to do basic short overviews of restorative for their staff to introduce them to the ideas and gauge how receptive people were.

THE LESSONS LEARNED

First, was having a deeper understanding of what a trauma-informed restorative school looked like. It is a combination of community-building/maintenance, problem-solving, and responding to harm. We also learned that the breakdown of time spent doing restorative is best when we spend about 60% building community, 30% collaboratively and proactively addressing unsolved problems, conflicts, or harm, and 10% addressing more serious interventions. A continuing myth schools fall into is that restorative is a method for dealing with discipline, rather than seeing it as a way of building community and creating culture. You cannot repair a community you did not build. The process of change is slow and is best not rushed. This change needs to be done with care and caution. Rushing the process tends to backfire. The more sustainable way is to go gradually and replace punitive systems with restorative, rather than trying to do too much all at once. This work is a marathon, not a sprint. Get yourself and your team ready for the long haul. Another lesson to realize is that you cannot community-build with students if you haven't done it with staff. What your staff do really does matter. Staff who are not modeling community will struggle to build community with students. We need to bring the five skills and circle process to staff. We need to see the practices in place with the adults before we try them with the students. It is also important to think about how large your school is and what resources you have. Implementing whole-school change involves training, policy changes, buy-in and support from multiple places, and this takes a budget to sustain the changes. Roll-out may involve the whole school all at once or a grade-by-grade approach.

Start with a team

First things first: Schools need to select the workgroup or implementation team who will get trained and begin the work in the school. Ideally, this needs to be made up of a small-to-medium size group of teachers, administrators, parents, and other school staff. Don't underestimate the power of the front-desk staff either, as these are some of the people in the school who have the most knowledge of how to make change happen. Front-desk staff often know parents, students, and staff and know how to connect those personalities into a community. Having school resource officers and security can be very beneficial. Having each voice in the school community represented on the team is vital to making sure every aspect has been considered. It works best to have all the voices the represent the community, and that includes those who might push back at us. They may have legitimate concerns that need to be heard.

The team, once formed, needs to get enough training to wrap their heads around the philosophy of restorative and a basic understanding of the skills and practices involved in restorative. This could be a basic two-day training or even something better like the intensive six-day training we did in several districts in Connecticut. Once teams have this understanding, they will be able to assess the readiness of the staff and the available resources to make the change. If the staff aren't behind this, it will be a challenge; and even if they are behind the change but there are no resources, that may also be a challenge. Do not just fill the team with folk who are on-board with restorative. I suggest inviting some of the nay-sayers, too. They have important concerns that need a voice on the team. Allowing those concerns to be heard and addressed may also help bring them round to becoming supporters. It is also important to focus some energy on learning about change management and implementation science. All too often schools use the "train and pray" system of change management, blindly thinking that because people are trained then change will follow. This rarely works the way it sounds. Just training staff will not make the systemic changes needed to support them having to do what they were trained to do. Change requires constant coaching and reinforcement of the material. It takes some nurturing to grow these changes, so this understanding moves from something inside people's heads and starts to take root in their hearts.

The biggest lesson

As the work in Connecticut, and a few other states where I was consulting, continued, I noticed that some schools were succeeding and others, even with the same supports, were failing to launch. Even when given the supports, the tools, the time to do the work, many schools were not doing well.

I had attended a few sessions at conferences where presenters talked about school readiness for change. I rarely had the opportunity to choose the schools in which I consulted and thought that it really did not matter if the school was ready or not if the leadership wanted to implement trauma-informed restorative practices. I maintained that stance until it was clear that readiness was the most logical explanation for why these schools were failing. They had experienced too much change in the years prior to trying to implement restorative. Staff with deeply rooted interpersonal conflicts can be distrustful of change. Unstable leadership was often a roadblock to success. In some failing schools, the staff had had four to five principals or administrators within three years, each coming in and making more and more changes. It became clear that readiness for change matters, so maybe it would be wise to assess readiness for change. Readiness for the change and implementation matters because implementation requires "all hands on deck." We need everyone in the building engaged in the work to make this change happen. Attrill, Thorsborne, and Turner (2019, p.27) write:

> It would seem a key component of a successful change process is the issue of engagement—engagement being the degree to which all members of the school community participate in the work of the implementation process—with dialogue, debate, trying new skills, decision-making, feedback. *We believe that even in the business of identifying the state of readiness of a school, that engagement of key stakeholders is fundamental to the process of implementation and its success.*

Attrill *et al.* (2019) suggest that three areas of assessment serve to address the readiness of a school for change: the Change Readiness Survey, the Relationship Survey and the Organizational Climate Survey. *Change Readiness Surveys* examine past initiatives as a predictor of how the next change process may go. Survey resources, roadblocks, and school conditions may impact the success of implementation. *Relationship Surveys* (sometimes referred to as "School Climate and Culture Surveys") are a way of measuring the school's relational ecology. Many of these surveys will measure family engagement, the school's fit for a child's developmental needs, school climate, school safety, and trust levels between students and staff. Understanding the quality of relationships in the school will help us to understand how the school will team up to own the implementation of this work. Typically, these surveys are filled out by the entire school community, including parents, students, and staff. Data from these surveys can help measure the state of the relationships and where they are broken and in need of healing. Always keep in mind that a trauma-informed school is a relationship-based school. *Organizational Climate Surveys* collect information from school staff on the direction from leadership, support for staff, respect levels, and consistency in expectations. These surveys can help to see any roadblocks that may exist in the relationships between staff and leadership; this is vital to the success of any change management in an organization.

When we have this background information on the state of the school culture, we can better assess whether we can jump right into our implementation of trauma-informed restorative practices or whether we have some pre-implementation work to do around relationships and overall school culture. In addition, this helps us use our limited resources more wisely, as dumping tons of funding into implementation when a school is not ready for change is not just a waste of money, it is also a waste of time.

Learning about influence and change

There are many change books on the market these days. Some of my favorites as a book addict are *Switch: How to Change When Change Is Hard* (Heath and Heath 2010) and *Leading Change* (Kotter 2012). As I have been implementing restorative in various school over the last few years, I have been finding that more emphasis needs to be put on the management of the change and the shift we are asking people to make. This change is both one of heart and one of structural process of how we do things in schools. We need to change people's hearts and we need to change referral forms, schedules to accommodate circles, suspension processes to include more reflection and re-entry circles, and budgets to implement both inside and outside training for staff. This change will be whole school and whole person.

Margaret Thorsborne and Peta Blood (2013), in their best-selling book *Implementing Restorative Practices in Schools: A Practical Guide to Transforming School Communities*, write (pp. 89–90):

> Major culture change initiatives bring with them interest, excitement, enjoyment for some, and a host of negative affects for others such

as distress, fear, anxiety and anger. Will I have a job? What will the requirements be? Will I have to change? How does this impact me? What does it mean in terms of my job satisfaction? Change that does not involve in meaningful dialogue and participation the very people affected by the change is doomed to fail. Without this, those that may have initially been excited by the change will start to doubt the process and turn against the initiative, no matter how much the implementers attempt to sidestep this process. Change is an emotional process.

THE SIX SOURCES OF INFLUENCE

I have learned we need to realize behavior has many more influences than just motivation. Just as we discussed children's behavior being a matter of skill, so is adult behavior. Just think of all the New Year's resolutions that people make and how many never follow through, even with their best intentions. It isn't lack of motivation. People are motivated to quit drinking, lose weight, quit smoking, etc. The question is what else influences their behavior beyond personal motivation? People are motivated to do these things, or they wouldn't have made a resolution. Why don't they succeed?

The answer to the above question can be found in *Change Anything: The New Science of Personal Success* (Patterson *et al.* 2011) and *Influencer: The Power to Change Anything* (Patterson *et al.* 2008). In each book, the authors introduce us to the Six Sources of Influence on either personal or systemic change. They claim that there are six powerful sources of influence on our behaviors and that when we are blind to what they are we struggle to make change. They also claim that when we harness at least four of the six, we better our chances of successful change tenfold. If we use all six, we are as good as guaranteed to make some changes in behavior. As I have been working with schools over the last few years, I keep finding myself returning to the Six Sources of Influence and how they make schools either succeed or fail at implementing various behaviors of restorative practice. It also keeps coming up in workshops and trainings, as the questions teachers and school staff ask me about include how to change a certain behavior, such as wearing hoodies or reducing cell phone use in the classroom. I find myself returning to the Six Sources of Influence from the *Influencer* and *Change Anything* models.

So, what is this model? The researchers at VitalSmarts looked at change-makers—people who had successfully influenced serious changes in the world; they then looked at what they had in common. For starters, they were all fans of Albert Bandura. I, for one, was happy to read this as I am a huge fan of Bandura's (1975) research and writing. Especially, they were fans of Bandura's (1977) Theory of Social Learning, which, at its core, says we are influenced heavily by watching each other's behaviors. This seems to be truer if we are talking about children's and adolescents' behavior influenced by adults. The team at VitalSmarts (Patterson *et al.* 2008, p.20) say something that backs this argument:

> [I]f you want others to change, you don't have to put them on a couch for 10 years to learn about their critical childhood moments. You also need not trouble yourself by laying out a trail of Reese's Pieces in front of others to propel them through a maze. Humans aren't simple-minded pawns who can be readily manipulated to do whatever you'd like—even if you have the right amount of candy.

These words stand as a testament to the fact that what we learned about children and adolescents in Section 1 will also apply to adults as we try to implement these ideas in schools. Teachers and school staff don't want to be manipulated into new behaviors like circle or mediation. They want support in making their schools better places of learning. How do we do that? The answer is in the same way we did with our youth: Stop judging them and start looking at the core roots of their behavior.

As humans we tend to make judgments about people's character and being, instead of looking at the core needs involved in their behaviors. This has been commonly referred to as "fundamental attribution error." I call it "fatal attribution error" because it cuts off our chances of life-serving connection. It is the basic idea that when someone does or doesn't do something and we believe they "should" or "shouldn't," it is a flaw in who they are. They didn't turn in their lesson plans because they are lazy. They didn't quieten down their class because they are incompetent. Of course, when we do the same things, the theory states we believe we had good reasons and it is not a flaw.

The other tendency is to judge another's behaviors as a lack of motivation, or what the team at VitalSmarts calls "The Will Power Trap." This is when we look at people's lack of success in changing as either not trying hard enough or they plain old just don't want to. We do this to ourselves too! Obviously, if we fail, we must not have wanted to change badly enough. Right? I have learned that it's not that simple.

Just as children's and adolescent's behavior is a matter of skill not will, the same applies to all of us. Ross Greene focused these ideas on children with challenging behavior, and the team at VitalSmarts pointed out that this applies to everyone. Human beings and their behaviors are not so simplistic that they can be swayed with simple carrot and stick mentality. If we want to make real lasting change in our school learning environments, we need to get clear about what is influencing our behaviors. We need to move away from B. F. Skinner's (1974) model of behaviorism and toward Bandura's (1977) Social Learning Theory. Honestly, I am amazed it is taking us so long to do it.

We need to focus on the vision of what our school will look like when we become trauma-informed and restorative. That means keeping in mind that there is no end or destination. It is a constant journey. There are some things we would like to see when our school transforms. What will we measure? What will meaningful results look like? The Appendix of this book offers you a checklist of what a trauma-informed restorative school looks like. What is the time frame? When will you get the results you are looking for?

When we start with the end in mind, it also means we will think about how to evaluate the change. This ensures we have a starting point for our data and allows us to use the data going forward to give feedback on what is and isn't working.

Our next step is to identify the vital behavior or what it is we want to change. When we focus on lowering suspensions, the problem is that isn't a behavior. Focusing on lowering suspensions doesn't tell people what behavior we want to change—it involves a change in the way administrators make decisions about handling serious issues. A great example from the book *Influencer: The Power to Change Anything* (Patterson *et al.* 2008) would be handwashing. If we want to lower infections in hospitals, we must focus on a behavior that is contributing to the problem. So, how do we get more people to wash their hands? Our focus isn't on the outcome of lowering infection; it is on the *behavior* that causes infections. One thing the VitalSmarts team points out about behaviors is to look at the positive deviance (Influencer Data), which means to look for the people in your school already succeeding and find out why. Look at the research and the stories of schools already doing restorative and trauma-informed work and find out what they did to succeed. You do not need to reinvent the wheel. While the team at VitalSmarts does go on to focus on some other ideas around behavior,

I want to jump right into the Six Sources of Influence (see Table 16.1) of behaviors and how I believe schools could benefit from being awake and alive to these powerful sources of change.

Table 16.1: The Six Sources of Influence

	Motivation	Ability
	Make the undesirable, desirable	Help them surpass their limits
Personal	Create new experiences: Let them experience circle, respect agreements, or Restorative Justice questions in person or have them watch a video. Spotlight human consequences to humanize data: Perhaps have staff tell some stories about their experiences in staff meetings. Connect Restorative Justice to staff values: Ask staff to reflect: "Is what I am doing meeting the intention of the values?"	Professional development schedules: Don't underestimate the power of training. Teach the Five Skills of Restorative. Break mastery into mini goals. Deliberate practice: Activities in staff meetings. Add feedback: Learning walks, checklists, feedback circles.
	Harness peer pressure	Find strength in numbers
Social	Enlist social support. Build the right team. Make the undiscussable, discussable: Use circle process to start having tough conversations.	Have the team train fellow staff. Use professional learning communities. Set up buddy systems to support use of practices and foster relational ecology.
	Design for accountability	Change the environment
Structural	Create positive consequences for using the practices: Talk up successes and show improved data. Create infrastructure to make doing this work rewarding.	Set up a permanent circle space. Set up a particular time for all classes to circle (e.g., advisory). Make the change unavoidable.

Source 1: Personal motivation

The first source of influence is personal motivation. All too often the behavior we are asking people to engage in is burdensome. Asking teachers to engage in Plan B takes time. Using time from the class day to do circles can be scary. Having a restorative dialogue with students can appear to be an extra duty. And serving on another team to plan another initiative can be overwhelming. It can be perceived that it is quicker to just suspend students and let their parents deal with them. Sadly, this approach does little to solve actual problems for students. If we want to increase personal motivation, the team at VitalSmarts offers us a few strategies.

The first strategy is to create new experiences with the behavior. It is a simple way of saying, "Just try it." Having teachers or staff participate in circle process, respect agreements, or a Plan B session can be a powerful way of bringing them on-board with these changes. If we can't get them to participate in a new process or behavior, perhaps we can get them to watch a circle or Plan B session. Perhaps we can get them to watch a video of a circle. We need to create an experience with restorative that is positive and allows them to change their thinking about what might happen to them if they try it. We need them to rethink the possibilities from negative (e.g., my class will descend into chaos or students will overshare) to the positive (e.g., students will be connecting with each other, or this student will be developing a relationship with me).

The team talks in the book *Influencer: The Power to Change Anything* (Patterson *et al.* 2008) about how people choose behaviors based on what they think will happen to them. Our mental stories have a huge impact. There is a big difference between staff believing "This will take away from teaching time," and "This will add to my teaching time." By giving them new experiences, we also help them reshape those mental stories.

Patterson *et al.* (2008) write that when we ask someone to do something—anything—before choosing to act or not act, the person will ask themselves two main questions:

"Is it worth it?"

"Can I do it?"

We try all sorts of things to get people to believe that the answer to these questions is "Yes." We try to verbally persuade with facts, which unfortunately fails most of the time. People don't just change their minds through verbal persuasion. If we want to change resistant people, the real mover and shaker is to get to their hearts—in other words, they need to experience an emotional shift when they participate in a restorative process—and this is what finally convinces many.

One way the authors suggest influencing the "Is it worth it?" answer for people is to put a spotlight on human consequences. We discussed in depth in Chapter 1 just how easy it is to disconnect our actions from the impacts they have. It's easy to suspend students when we disconnect ourselves from what they might be doing to their well-being or do not consider "their story behind the story." Sometimes we need the data to come to life. This is of the reasons why I have chosen not to focus on zero tolerance policies or suspension data in this book. I want to focus on humanizing the data into real-life people and situations.

I can't even begin to tell you the stories I have heard time and time again from teachers who attend a circle training with me and then come back to tell me about their first attempt at restorative. While some of those stories say it didn't go well, most of them tell me how amazing it was. Bringing educators on-board with restorative is much easier when they get a chance to try it, especially if it is a restorative circle that addressed the harm caused by a student and is followed by healing.

The next strategy the VitalSmarts team talks about is one of my favorites to increase personal motivation: story/narrative. We talked earlier in this book and in this chapter about narrative and story and the influence these have on school culture. In their work, the authors talk about how we create "profound vicarious experiences" by using story to motivate people (Patterson *et al.* 2008, p.53). When we look at the history of social change in the USA on big issues such as gay rights, abortion, single mothers, addiction and recovery, mental illness, etc., we often see how change has been greatly influenced by powerful characters in books and on television and radio programs. These characters personalized and humanized tough issues by giving them a face. We had *Maude* (airing from 1972 to 1978), a liberal feminist character played by actress Bea Arthur, who gave a face and a personal story to abortion at a time when that subject matter was simply unspeakable. We had the show *All in the Family* (airing from 1971 to 1979), where Archie Bunker's conservative and sometimes ignorant views of social issues would be personally challenged as he met Blacks, gays, and others who didn't fit his stereotypes of what these people "should" look like. More recently on TV, *Parenthood* gave us characters that informed and allowed us to empathize with a family member living with autism, and *The Fosters* challenged our views about sexuality, same-sex parenting, and even addiction and recovery. In both the UK and the USA, we had programs like *Shameless*, which highlighted the struggle of generational trauma as we followed a young woman left to raise her younger brothers and sisters in the face of addiction and poverty. These characters got us to personalize issues we might otherwise feel completely disconnected from in our daily lives. This is what we need to do with

Restorative Justice in schools. We need to connect people to stories that humanize this work in a way data and statistics can't. We need to tell stories and celebrate successes as we have them; perhaps have teachers talk about their stories of using restorative in their classrooms at each staff meeting or share them in a monthly newsletter.

Another way for us to create profound vicarious experience is school-wide reading. Many schools across the USA are asking their students and staff to read *Touching Spirit Bear* (Mikaelsen 2005), about a 15-year-old boy struggling with his experiences with the law, his alcoholic parents, and his parole officer. After an incident where the main character, Cole, is sent into a Restorative Justice circle for beating up a fellow student, the book follows both Cole and the student he has harmed through their process of healing because of the outcomes of the circle. In one school doing this work, the 5th to 8th grades are all reading this book together. Students are having deep discussions about circle justice, healing, alcohol, and other issues, which are all humanized by the characters in the book. An entire hallway bulletin board has been devoted to meeting the characters. It is worth noting that these discussions happen in circle. It gives both students and teachers some shared language around these new experiences.

Having staff-wide book clubs can also be a successful way of helping to support and manage the change process. *Implementing Restorative Practice in Schools: A Practical Guide to Transforming School Communities* by Thorsborne and Blood (2013) or *Influencer: The Power to Change Anything* (Patterson *et al.* 2008) are great choices. Staff could also form book groups that could present executive summaries to the staff as a way of getting through the huge mounds of resources that exist for schools to do this work.

I am not someone who typically takes a highlighter pen to my books. I did do it with the book *Influencer: The Power to Change Anything* (Patterson *et al.* 2008) and highlighted the following paragraph (p.61):

> Concrete and vivid stories exert extraordinary influence because they transport people out of the role of critic and into the role of participant. The more poignant, vibrant, and relevant the story, the more the listener moves from thinking about the inherent arguments to experiencing every element of the take itself. Stories don't merely trump verbal persuasion by disproving counterarguments; stories keep the listener from offering counterarguments in the first place.

If we want to make change using personal motivation, we may want to combine storytelling with creating new experiences. I believe role-plays of actual circles that also have real stories behind them do that. Don't be afraid to go beyond just telling staff about a successful circle; have them role-play the experience of it.

It is important to say again that personal motivation isn't enough to create change. Thousands of people across the globe are motivated to get in-shape, eat healthy, and work out on a more regular basis. Being motivated isn't enough. We need the next source of influence, and that is personal ability. Wanting to swim isn't the same as knowing how to swim.

Source 2: Personal ability

Patterson *et al.* (2008) propose that the second source of influence is personal ability, otherwise known as skill. This is no different to what Ross Greene (2014a), whose work we discussed in Section 2, is saying when he states that children are motivated to do well and that it is a matter of skill not motivation that gets in the way.

When we want to influence change, we must acknowledge that skills and ability are just as important as the desire to make the change. People prefer doing well in the world. No one, neither child nor adult, prefers doing poorly. So why do people sometimes not make changes in their behavior? It is because they don't always know how. They lack personal ability, not motivation. Think about this one: If you want to lose weight, even desperately, you are motivated. Do you know about nutrition? Do you know how to calculate calorie intake? If not, motivation alone won't help you lose any weight. You need skills.

Personal ability also goes beyond training. The world of education has depended on the "train and pray" model of implementation for years. It often fails at getting programs off the ground because just training teachers in these practices isn't enough to make people start using them. It is one part of personal ability. We need to add practice. We need to add coaching. We need to add feedback. We also need to add resilience and coping skills for failure for when we have a circle of practice that doesn't work out.

Deliberate practice

Surprisingly, doing something for a long time doesn't make you better at it. Repetition isn't the same as practice. Improvement comes from purposely trying to get better at something. Consider how we teach children to learn musical instruments. We don't just tell them to play a lot. We tell them to practice scales. We give them specific exercises to practice that develop certain aspects of their playing. It makes sense to give them such deliberate practice to develop their talents. Why wouldn't we do this for other new skills? For example, having students practice telling a bully to stop harassing them or having teachers role-play difficult conversations with parents so they can learn better communication skills. If we wanted to get little ones to wash their hands before eating a snack, wouldn't we want them to practice how we want them to do it, so it is effective?

Add feedback

Practice gets better and more useful when it comes with immediate feedback. For years, I have been training people to be mediators using role-plays of conflict scenarios. At the end of each role-play, either I or a coach who volunteered will give feedback to training participants on what went well. We also encourage them to self-reflect on their performance as mediators, offering themselves some feedback on what went well and what could be improved.

Teachers and staff will need feedback on their circle skills. They will want feedback on their Plan B sessions.[1] People always need to debrief restorative process to see where they can improve. Having feedback is even better if it is done according to some type of standard. People need to know how they stack up against a standard. It can be criteria or guidelines. Try to have some type of compass of how well people are doing. This is the space where you will need to make sure trainings are supporting the practices and that policy changes are coordinated with the practices you roll out. Start thinking from the start of your implementation how you will evaluate the work. Waiting until three years into the implementation to ask "Is this working?" is too late.

Another suggestion the team at VitalSmarts talks about is breaking mastery into mini goals. Having a roll-out plan of at least three years

---

1   Resources for Plan B and Collaborative and Proactive Solutions are available at www. livesinthebalance.org.

with ideas about how you can celebrate little victories is vital to change. Perhaps year one is when you roll out circles and restorative dialogue, and year two is when you roll out Collaborative and Proactive Solutions, all the while asking and polling staff and students on how this is working for them. What is working and what is not? We can use our three-year plan to break the totality of this work into smaller goals year by year. Looking at all these skills, practices, and infrastructural change can be overwhelming until you break it into smaller, bite-sized pieces broken down by year. When, in year one we think something isn't doable, add the word "yet" to that: "It isn't doable, yet." It could be doable if you planned thinking long-term, not short-term.

Source 3: Social motivation

A major source of influence for teachers is other teachers. As we look to motivate teachers, we often overlook just how much they impact each other. People can be personally motivated and do have the ability to complete what we are asking. They can believe it's worth it and they can do it. Then comes the influence of what others are doing. If some staff members are walking around talking about how they are not doing circles, they don't have time for restorative dialogue, or that punishment is needed for compliance, it's unlikely we can push them to try anything restorative. We need teachers and staff to motivate each other. Telling stories of success is one way of doing this. Start every staff meeting with some success stories of circles or successful Plan B sessions. We need the motivation and inspiration of each staff member to help motivate and inspire other staff members. These stories make it safer for those who are reluctant or lack confidence to have a go. Peer pressure works for adults too!

One way to build social motivation (and ability) is to use professional learning communities. This could include book clubs, movie nights, trainings, and professional development. In a school we discussed earlier, all students and teachers were reading the book *Touching Spirit Bear* by Ben Mikaelsen (2005). The book introduced both staff and students to the ideas of restorative circle. Each classroom had bulletin boards showing character studies and exploration of the restorative philosophy. This gave both staff and students a chance to wrap their heads around these concepts and do it as a community. The bulletin boards acted as daily reminders that this was the direction the school was going in.

Another way to build social motivation is to build the right team with the right players. Make sure you have found a few social movers and shakers. Build a team with members who already influence other teachers. Be sure to tap a few staff members who don't agree with you or have concerns. These are the people who make change when they see that their concerns matter and will be addressed.

Use circle process to start having tough discussions in your school. These might include staff members not feeling supported; these might be tough discussions about racism and equity. Sometimes this can be done through stories about real humans and the tough issues, activities that bridge the subjects that need discussion, or just prompting questions to the circle that allow people to discuss things that are often unpopular topics for discussion.

Source 4: Social ability

It is also important for us to look at how we enable each other to do or not do restorative in schools. Social ability refers to how staff support each other or make these practices doable. Are you personally motivated and do you have the ability? Are you socially motivated by your peers? Do your peers help you or prevent you from using the skills and practices? A simple example of this is a restorative chat/dialogue. This will require staff to have the time to meet with a student. Often, I see that paraprofessional or behavior specialists are called to a classroom to pull a student out and help them with a behavior problem in class. What if the specialist didn't take the student out and instead managed the class while the teacher worked with the student? This is one way we gain social ability—having others support our use of the tools rather than getting in our way.

This is an important place for administrative teams to understand how much influence they have. Just personally motivating staff with stories and training is never going to be enough. We also need to support staff. This means making a few schedule adjustments, and providing administrative supports, time, substitute teachers, and money. Staff need to make these changes possible for each other and this includes covering each other's classes, possibly teaming up to get training, and lessening each other's workload to make the changes possible.

How will staff support each other in the use of vital behaviors like circle, restorative chats, or Plan B? Unlike our current Western culture where hyper-individualism is promoted as the way people succeed, restorative reminds us constantly that no one succeeds alone in the world. Successful people have teams behind them making things happen. The same is true of the successful implementation of ideas, programs, and models in education. We need the whole building working toward the goal. We want to embrace those who are struggling and make sure resources are shared in ways that enable the ability to do the practices.

Source 5: Structural motivation

It's quite surprising how much the environment can motivate us to act. Signs, posters, wall paint, music, lighting, and furniture are all factors that influence us to do things. I always remind people of the brilliance in the design of an Ikea store. There is one in my town and to navigate the store you follow a path, guided by arrows on the floor that are projected from above. The arrows direct you through the store, almost forcing you to browse each department. Of course, this design wants you to buy more products, or at best to look at them. The same is true when you truck to the grocery store and wonder how you went in to buy bread and milk and came out later having spent $200. Strategic things go into the placement of products, the music you hear in the background, and the color choices in the store. All the choices are psychologically made to motivate you to make purchases.

We need to apply the same strategic thinking to our schools. Putting lines down the center of the hallway with arrows may help students walk the halls without bumping into each other. Calm colors with warm lights in our de-escalation room might get students to lower their stress levels. Having a space in the school where a circle is already set up can help to encourage people to circle up.

We need to create a space that motivates us to use restorative in a trauma-informed space. We need posters reminding staff and students to use the restorative questions and restorative dialogue and to be mindful; we even need posters promoting restorative around the school. We want both staff and students to be aware of, and have ownership over, a trauma-informed and restorative school.

Source 6: Structural ability

Does the space we are in allow for circle? Are the lab tables nailed to the floor? Do we have a space for a calm room? It is surprising just how often we want to do things. We are motivated to do them, yet the space won't allow for it. We need to change the environment, so we can encourage trauma-informed Restorative Justice. We need spaces to create relationships.

I was once working in a school that was going through a remodel. The gym was not ready, so they couldn't have big pep rallies. The auditorium was also unfinished, so no school play was possible that year. The space didn't allow for those things. The school climate took a hit without those crucial methods of creating and maintaining the relational ecology. The school just lacked the structural ability to create community in the ways that it had done in the past.

Structural ability is how we make things possible by making them easier to do. For instance, we can put up posters to motivate people to wash their hands and we can tell stories about how handwashing is so important to health. We can have staff encourage and make time for other staff members to wash their hands. If, after all that, there are no handwashing stations, then we have a structural issue blocking ability. We need our structural set-up to allow for the vital behaviors we are seeking. If we want circle, does the schedule allow for a circle? If we want to track restorative, does the referral form have a check-box for restorative chats? Does the referral form allow for circles?

Make the change unavoidable. Hold staff meetings in circle. Take staff time to create a staff-to-staff respect agreement that is utilized as a communication tool. Have the referral documentation ask about what restorative practices have been tried. Have leadership model trauma-informed practices every day. Include a mindfulness activity in the morning announcements. Make the switch to restorative as part of the day-to-day fabric of the school.

CREATING THE THREE-YEAR PLAN

When we can bring these Six Sources of Influence into our actions plans to roll out restorative, we can then see the barriers and/or promoters in our personal, social, and environmental influencers that either support the change we are making or prevent the change.

Implementation of this work needs to be a bottom-up, top-down, side-to-side approach (see Figure 16.1). From the top down, we need administrators and leadership to guide the process for purposes of funding, policy changes, and a review of school conduct codes to make sure they are restorative, equitable, and anti-racist. This may involve schedule changes to allow for circles and Plan B sessions to occur.

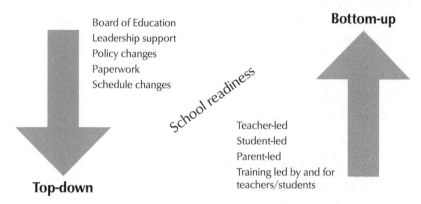

Figure 16.1: Implementation

We also need the effort to be teacher-led, student-driven, and parent-approved. We need as much of the work as we can to be an inside job. No one knows this school and its community better than the people in it. We need the implementation team to lead the training work, coupled with outside trainings, conferences, and books, movies, or consultants who can coach the process. This ensures the work is being done "with" staff not "to" them or "for" them as we discussed in Section 1.

The creation of a three-year plan is vital to hold everyone accountable for doing the work needed for change and to make sure training happens in ways that support the various practices being rolled out. The plan works best when it remains a three-year plan. When a year is finished, we add another year and keep planning. There is no end point with this work! It can always go deeper. Keep in mind that each new school year brings new students, new parents, and sometimes new staff. Our work is never "done." As the three-year plan is created, it needs to focus on what will happen when. It is important to look at what changes need to happen and when they need to happen. Coordinating those two things is key. Don't train staff on circles while requiring them to do respect agreements. Line it up!

Your plan will be holistic if you include four main elements for each year of the plan: systems changes; physical changes to the building; procedural changes about how policy is enacted; and a training/professional development plan for each of the areas you are concentrating on with each year. For example, if year one includes the implementation of circles, then professional development in the different types of circles would be suggested.

As you build the plan, be sure to build in accountability. How will you know who is responsible for what and when? It is helpful to add into that the thinking of "not yet," which simply means that maybe we can't do something in year one due to funding issues. That means it is a "not yet," instead of a "not at all." It means you have the opportunity to use year one to look for funding for those things in the upcoming years.

THREE-YEAR PLAN NEEDS

Systems changes
Code of conduct
Board of Education
Community partners
Union partnership

Physical changes
Building safety
Classroom declutter
Posters
De-escalation space

Procedural changes
Forms and paperwork
Referral forms
Schedule
Circles
Policy versus procedure

Professional development
Five Skills of Restorative
Trauma
Restorative Justice library of resources
Outside versus inside training

Build in accountability

Figure 16.2: Three-year plan

✳ ✳ ✳

As we reach the end of this chapter, our next and final chapter will help to bring all these ideas into one space. The Conclusion will help connect the dots that haven't already been connected about just how these ideas, practices, philosophies, and skills overlap in such significant ways. When we can connect these dots, it means we can have a bigger picture of possibility for our schools, our communities, and ultimately for a better world for our children.

Conclusion

This book has been a labor of love and healing. The hope is that by now you see some of what I have found in my journey. The possibility that structuring schools to be trauma-informed and restorative will increase the quality of life of everyone because we can have less trauma impacting our future. I also hope that you now see how combining the implementation of the ideas will also make it easier, less expensive, and less stressful for school staff.

In Section 1 we spent time learning about the "why" of this work. We learned that motivation-based interventions only work for children who don't need them and fail the ones who do. We learned the powerful notion that what children need isn't stickers or suspensions. They need executive function skills and self-regulation. We explored how trauma plays a role in the development of those skills and the ability of schools to teach. We also saw how trauma influences our futures by creating addicts, breaking apart relationships, preventing learning, and filling our prisons with hurting people. We examined the studies that show how trauma impairs our health and social outcomes. Ultimately, we learned we need to change what we are doing because it clearly is not working.

Section 2 introduced a set of skills. We explored how those skills could improve our ability to connect with each other and the children we seek to educate. We learned how asking the deeper questions, being present enough to hear the answers, and speaking our truth without blame or judgment help us to stay trauma-informed and restorative. Along with that, we learned what it takes to ask those who are responsible for causing harm to repair the harm from a strengths-based, non-punitive, and healing way using restorative S.S.M.A.R.T goals.

Section 3 let us explore what these ideas look like in practice. Like any practice, it takes time to reach mastery. The third section offered us practical things to "do" in schools to help us live out this way of "being" in the world. We looked at how using restorative language school-wide can create a safer and more trauma-informed environment for everyone. If we are going to be a trauma-informed school, we also need to be a trauma-informed workplace. Our language matters in doing that.

Section 3 also looked at circle process, respect agreements, and regulation spaces such as peace corners to support better behavior from students and a better culture all around. We also took a brief look at Collaborative and Proactive Solutions as a new way of handling challenging behavior in preventive ways.

In Section 4, we also explored how to make change happen. This section reminded you that change in a school is an inside job. No one can do it "for" you, and leadership can't do it "to" you. This work needs to be implemented with the same principles and values that it seeks to put into your school. It is teaching, leading, and showing up for our communities from the "with" box of the Relationship Matrix. Section 4 was a reminder that all around us are sources of influence that can sway our behaviors to do or not do something in our lives.

As we approach the end of this book, which I hope is the beginning of your journey, I hope you will take the next steps of attending a training or conference, starting a trauma-informed restorative book club at your school, or combing your way through the bibliography of this book and start reading. Having trauma-informed restorative schools isn't the end of the road. It *is* the road. The end is healthy communities.

This work is built on the "values of respect, dignity, and mutual concern, based on the core belief that all people are worthy of being honored and valued" (Gregory and Evans 2020, p.8). To truly implement this work into your school community, there are some core principles we need to follow:

1. **Leave people better than you found them:** This is the equivalent of the age-old mantra, "do no harm." As we dive into this work, we will encounter lots of souls, some who are thriving and improving all the time, and some who are struggling to get through the day. Do your best to leave them in circumstances, conditions, and a state that is better than the one you found them in. If this is not possible, then don't make things worse.

2. **Trauma is prevalent:** The effects of trauma on our society are everywhere around us (Souers and Hall 2016). Our prisons are filled with people impacted by trauma. Our addiction clinics

are filled with people impacted by trauma. This needs to be the lens through which we see everything else we do. While trauma is prevalent, resilience could be as well.

3. **Intersectionality and racial justice need to be drivers:** We need to acknowledge in this work that historical and ongoing oppression based on race, sex, gender expression, religion, sexual orientation, class, and ability are forms of trauma. Our work needs to concentrate on repairing the harms done by oppression and preventing those harms by actively dismantling the systems that perpetuate those harms going forward.

4. **Trauma-informed restorative schools are relationship-based:** Our schools and communities need to abandon the ethos of hyper-individualism, abandoning the "I" way of thinking for more "we" in our thinking. In African wisdom, this is named *Ubuntu*. It means that "I am because we are, and we are because I am" (Davis 2019, p.17). It is a reminder that human beings heal from trauma in the safety and trust of the relationships around them. This is why relational ecology in our schools is so important. We need to continue to uphold the idea that building, maintaining, and repairing relationships are core to this work. It means we need to foster relationships and have conflict resolution plans in place for when those relationships are in jeopardy.

5. **Safety is non-negotiable:** To get students out of their stress response systems and into the parts of the brain that allow them to learn new information, we need to make students feel confident in their own safety, both emotionally and physically.

6. **Everyone is doing the best they can:** To remind us of Ross Greene's (2014b) mantra, "Kids do well if they can" (p.10), let's also remember, this is true of adults. Everyone is doing the best they can with the skills they've got, in the circumstances they have. We all mess it up sometimes, and for some of us, the mess is worse than for others. We are all still worthy of love and belonging.

7. **We are all interconnected, whether we choose to acknowledge it or not:** What one of us does impacts all of us. We do not live in a vacuum, and our actions or lack thereof impact others.

8. **Trustworthiness and transparency:** The idea of trustworthiness and transparency, from the Substance Abuse and Mental Health Services Administration (US Department of Health and Human Services 2014), is added here because this is how organizations need to act to be trauma-informed. Decisions in our communities and schools are made transparently and with a goal to build and maintain trust. Where appropriate, we need to be transparent in how and why decisions are made. We need to do our best to include the voices of those who will be impacted by a decision in the process of that decision. This maintains and builds trust and better-quality relationships.

9. **Responding to harms requires the voices of those harmed:** It is imperative that the voices of all stakeholders involved in an incident in our schools or communities be included in the repair of harm. To leave out a voice is to further the harm. Invitation to the table and a voice at that table are ways of honoring the hurt the person has suffered.

10. **Respect is the default:** Everyone's life has value and wisdom worthy of our respect. It doesn't need to be earned. Respect is given as a way of honoring the life force in others. It is just as much about who others are when they receive respect, as who you are when you offer it. Offering respect to others when they "don't seem to deserve it" is to honor their potential to change and to be their best self in the future.

Strangely, what is helpful and necessary for the most vulnerable amongst us also happens to be helpful for the rest of us. Remember that as you move forward with this work.

References

Attrill, S., Thorsborne, M. and Turner, B. (2019) 'Assessing Readiness for Restorative Practice Implementation.' In M. Thorsborne, N. Riestenberg and G. McCluskey (eds.) *Getting More Out of Restorative Practices: Practical Approaches to Improve School Wellbeing and Strengthen Community Engagement.* London: Jessica Kingsley Publishers.

Avildsen, J. G. (Director) (1984) *The Karate Kid* [Motion Picture]. United States of America: Sony.

Bandura, A. (1977) *Social Learning Theory.* Englewood Cliffs, NJ: Prentice Hall.

Bandura, A., Underwood, B. and Fromson, M. E. (1975) 'Disinhibition of aggression through diffusion of responsibility and dehumanization of victims.' *Journal of Research in Personality 9,* 253–269.

Bloom, S. (1997) *Creating Sanctuary: Toward an Evolution of Sane Societies.* New York, NY: Routledge.

Boyes-Watson, C. and Pranis, K. (2015) *Circle Forward: Building a Restorative School Community.* St. Paul, MN: Living Justice Press.

Brown, B. (2007) *I Thought It Was Just Me (but it isn't): Telling the Truth About Perfectionism, Inadequacy, and Power.* New York, NY: Gotham Books.

Brown, B. (2010) *The Gifts of Imperfection: Let Go of Who You Think You're Supposed to Be and Embrace Who You Are.* Center City, MN: Hazelden.

Brown, B. (2012) *Daring Greatly: How the Courage to Be Vulnerable Transforms the Way We Live, Love, Parent, and Lead* [Kindle version]. New York, NY: Gotham.

Brown, M. (2018) *Creating Restorative Schools: Setting Schools Up to Succeed.* St. Paul, MN: Living Justice Press.

Brummelman, E., Thomaes, S., Overbecek, G., de Castro, B., van den Hout, M. and Bushman, B. J. (2014) 'On feeding those hungry for praise: Person praise backfires in children with low self-esteem.' *Journal of Educational Psychology, 143*(1), 9–14.

Burke-Harris, N. (2018) *The Deepest Well: Healing the Long-Term Effects of Childhood Adversity.* Boston, MA: Mariner.

Caplan, A. (2015) *Trauma and Restorative Practices in Schools.* Accessed on 2020/3/19 at https://prezi.com/wzftai4_9zit/trauma-and-restorative-practices-in-schools.

Centers for Disease Control and Prevention (2019) *About the CDC-Kaiser ACE Study.* Accessed on 2020/25/1 at www.cdc.gov/violenceprevention/childabuseandneglect/acestudy/about.html.

Claassen, R. and Claassen, R. (2008) *Discipline That Restores: Strategies to Create Respect, Cooperation, and Responsibility in the Classroom.* Charleston, SC: Booksurge Publishing.

Costello, B., Wachtel, J. and Wachtel, T. (2009) *The Restorative Practices Handbook for Teachers, Disciplinarians and Administrators* [Kindle version]. Bethlehem, PA: International Institute for Restorative Practices.

Crawford, D. K., Bodine, R. J. and Hoglund, R. G. (1993) *The School for Quality Learning: Managing the School and Classroom the Deming Way*. Champaign, IL: Research Press.

d'Ansembourg, T. (2007) *Being Genuine: Stop Being Nice, Start Being Real*. Encinitas, CA: PuddleDancer Press.

Davis, F. E. (2019) *The Little Book of Race and Restorative Justice*. New York, NY: Good Books.

Deci, E. and Flaste, R. (1995) *Why We Do What We Do: Understanding Self-Motivation* (2nd ed.). New York, NY: Penguin Books.

De Waal, F. (2009) *The Age of Empathy: Nature's Lessons for a Kinder Society*. New York, NY: Crown Publishing.

Doran, G. T. (1981) 'There's a S.M.A.R.T. way to write management's goals and objectives.' *Management Review 70*(11), 35–36.

Evans, K. and Vaandering, D. (2016) *The Little Book of Restorative Justice in Education: Fostering Responsibility, Healing, and Hope in Schools*. New York, NY: Skyhorse Publishing.

Follestad, B. and Wroldsen, N. (2019) *Using Restorative Circles in Schools: How to Build Strong Learning Communities and Foster Student Wellbeing*. London: Jessica Kingsley Publishers.

Forbes, H. (2012) *Help for Billy: A Beyond Consequences Approach to Helping Challenging Children in the Classroom*. Boulder, CO: Beyond Consequences Institute.

Glasser, W. (1998) *Choice Theory: A New Psychology of Personal Freedom* [Kindle version]. New York, NY: HarperCollins.

Goleman, D. (2007) Three Kinds of Empathy. Accessed on 2020/31/1 at www.danielgoleman. info/three-kinds-of-empathy-cognitive-emotional-compassionate.

Greene, R. W. (2008) *Lost at School: Why Our Kids with Behavioral Challenges are Falling Through the Cracks and How We Can Help Them*. New York, NY: Scribner.

Greene, R. W. (2014a) *The Explosive Child: A New Approach for Understanding and Parenting Easily Frustrated, Chronically Inflexible Children* [Kindle version]. New York, NY: Harper.

Greene, R. W. (2014b) Lost at School: Why Our Kids with Behavioral Challenges are Falling Through the Cracks and How We Can Help Them [Kindle version]. New York, NY: Scribner.

Gregory, A. and Evans, K. R. (2020) *The Starts and Stumbles of Restorative Justice in Education: Where Do We Go from Here?* Boulder, CO: National Education Policy Center. Accessed on 2020/6/2 at http://nepc.colorado.edu/publication/restorative-justice.

Hanh, T. N. (1991) *Peace Is Every Step: The Path of Mindfulness in Everyday Life*. New York, NY: Bantam Books.

Harvard University, Center on the Developing Child (n.d.) *Executive Function and Self-Regulation*. Accessed on 2020/25/1 at https://developingchild.harvard.edu/science/key-concepts/executive-function.

Heath, C. and Heath, D. (2010) *Switch: How to Change When Change is Hard*. New York, NY: Crown Publishing Group.

Kelly, V. and Thorsborne, M. (eds.) (2014) *The Psychology of Emotion in Restorative Practice: How Effect Script Psychology Explains How and Why Restorative Practice Works*. London: Jessica Kingsley Publishers.

Kohn, A. (1993) *Punished by Rewards: The Trouble with Gold Stars, Incentive Plans, A's, Praise, and Other Bribes*. Boston, MA: Houghton Mifflin.

Kohn, A. (1994, December) *The Risk of Rewards* (ERIC Document Reproduction Service No. ED376990). Accessed on 2020/25/1 at www.alfiekohn.org/article/risks-rewards.

Kohn, A. (2006) *Unconditional Parenting: Moving from Rewards and Punishments to Love and Reason* [Kindle version]. New York, NY: Atria Books.

Kohn, A. (2016, September 7) 'On punishment for bullying – and punishment as bullying.' *Education Week*. Accessed on 2020/24/1 at www.alfiekohn.org/article/punishment-bullying.

Kotter, J. (2012) *Leading Change*. Boston, MA: Harvard Business Review Press.

Leu, L. (2003) *Nonviolent Communication Companion Workbook: A Practical Guide for Individuals, Group, or Classroom Study*. Encinitas, CA: PuddleDancer Press.

Littky, D. (2004) *The Big Picture: Education Is Everyone's Business*. Alexandria, VA: Association for Supervision and Curriculum Development.

Markham, L. (2019) *Why Punishment Doesn't Teach Your Child Accountability*. Accessed on 2020/25/1 at www.ahaparenting.com/blog/Why_Punishment_Doesnt_Teach_Your_Child_Accountability.

Maslow, A. H. (1943) 'A theory of human motivation.' *Psychological Review 50*(4), 370–396.

Middlebrooks J. S. and Audage N. C. (2008) *The Effects of Childhood Stress on Health across the Lifespan*. Atlanta (GA): Centers for Disease Control and Prevention, National Center for Injury Prevention and Control. Accessed on 2020/2/3 at https://stacks.cdc.gov/view/cdc/6978.

Mikaelsen, B. (2005) *Touching Spirit Bear* [Kindle version]. New York, NY: HarperCollins.

Mulvahill, E. (2018) *Understanding Intrinsic vs. Extrinsic Motivation in the Classroom: What's the Magic Formula?* Accessed on 2020/24/1 at www.weareteachers.com/understanding-intrinsic-vs-extrinsic-motivation-in-the-classroom.

Newberg, A. and Waldman, M. R. (2006) *Why We Believe What We Believe: Uncovering Our Biological Need for Meaning, Spirituality, and Truth*. New York, NY: Free Press.

Oakland Unified School District (n.d.) *Restorative Justice Implementation Guide: A Whole School Approach*. Accessed on 2020/6/2 at www.ousd.org/Page/1054.

Oprah Winfrey Network (2012, May 6) *Thich Nhat Hanh on Compassionate Listening* [Video file]. Accessed on 2020/1/24 at www.youtube.com/watch?v=lyUxYflkhzo.

O'Shaughnessy, A. (2019) 'Transforming Teaching and Learning through Mindfulness-Based Restorative Practices.' In M. Thorsborne, N. Riestenberg and G. McCluskey (eds.) *Getting More Out of Restorative Practices: Practical Approaches to Improve School Wellbeing and Strengthen Community Engagement*. London: Jessica Kingsley Publishers.

Patterson, K., Grenny, J., Maxfield, D., McMillan, R. and Switzler, A. (2008) *Influencer: The Power to Change Anything*. New York, NY: McGraw-Hill.

Patterson, K., Grenny, J., Maxfield, D., McMillan, R. and Switzler, A. (2011) *Change Anything: The New Science of Personal Success*. New York, NY: VitalSmarts.

Pink, D. (2009) *Drive: The Surprising Truth about What Motivates Us*. New York, NY: Riverhead Books.

Pritzker, K. (Producer), Scully, R. K. (Producer) and Redford, J. (2015) *Paper Tigers* [Motion picture]. United States of America: Passion River Studios.

Public Counsel (n.d.) *Fix School Discipline: How We Can Fix School Discipline Toolkit for Educators*. Accessed on 2020/2/1 at https://view.joomag.com/fix-school-discipline-toolkit-for-educators/0264187001429224353?short.

Riestenberg, N. (2012) *Circle in the Square: Building Community and Repairing Harm in School* [Kindle version]. St. Paul, MN: Living Justice Press.

Robbins, T. (2006, February) *Why We Do What We Do* [Video file]. Accessed on 2020/25/1 at www.ted.com/talks/tony_robbins_why_we_do_what_we_do.

Rosenberg, M. (2003a) *Life-Enriching Education: Nonviolent Communication Helps Schools Improve Performance, Reduce Conflict, and Enhance Relationships*. Encinitas, CA: PuddleDancer Press.

Rosenberg, M. (2003b) *Nonviolent Communication: A Language of Life*. Encinitas, CA: PuddleDancer Press.

Rosenberg, M. (2004) *The Heart of Social Change: How to Make a Difference in the World*. Encinitas, CA: PuddleDancer Press.

Rosenberg, M. (2015) *Nonviolent Communication: A Language of Life* (3rd ed.). Encinitas, CA: PuddleDancer Press.

Santorelli, S. F. (2014) *Mindfulness-Based Stress Reduction (MBSR): Standards of Practice.* Accessed on 2020/5/1 at www.umassmed.edu/contentassets/24cd221488584125835 e2eddce7dbb89/mbsr_standards_of_practice_2014.pdf.

Sege, R. D. and Siegel, B. S. (2018) 'Effective discipline to raise healthy children.' *Pediatrics* 142(6), e20183112.

Siegel, D. J. (2013) *Brainstorm: The Power and Purpose of the Teenage Brain.* New York, NY: Penguin Books.

Siegel, D. J. and Payne-Bryson, T. (2011) *The Whole-Brain Child: 12 Revolutionary Strategies to Nurture Your Child's Developing Mind* [Kindle version]. New York, NY: Delacorte Press.

Siegel, D. J. and Payne-Bryson, T. (2014) *No-Drama Discipline: The Whole-Brain Way to Calm the Chaos and Nurture Your Child's Developing Mind* [Kindle version]. New York, NY: Bantam Books.

Siegel, D. J. and Payne-Bryson, T. (2015) *The Whole-Brain Child Workbook: Practical Exercises, Worksheets and Activities to Nurture Developing Minds.* Eau Claire, WI: Random House Publishing Group.

Skinner, B. F. (1974) *About Behaviorism.* New York, NY: Knopf.

Sorrels, B. (2015) *Reaching and Teaching Children Exposed to Trauma.* Lewisville, NC: Gryphon House.

Souers, K. and Hall, P. (2016) *Fostering Resilient Learners: Strategies for Creating a Trauma-Sensitive Classroom.* Alexandria, VA: Association for Supervision and Curriculum Development.

Sporleder, J. and Forbes, H. T. (2016) *The Trauma-Informed School: A Step-by-Step Implementation Guide for Administrators and School Personnel.* Boulder, CO: Beyond Consequences Institute.

Stevens, J. E. (2013) *Nearly 35 million U.S. children have experienced one or more types of childhood trauma.* Accessed on 2020/19/3 at https://acestoohigh.com/2013/05/13/nearly-35-million-u-s-children-have-experienced-one-or-more-types-of-childhood-trauma.

Thorsborne, M. and Blood, P. (2013) *Implementing Restorative Practice in Schools: A Practical Guide to Transforming School Communities* [Kindle version]. London: Jessica Kingsley Publishers.

U.S. Department of Health and Human Services, Substance Abuse and Mental Health Services Administration (2014) *SAMHSA's Concept of Trauma and Guidance for a Trauma-Informed Approach.* Accessed on 2020/6/2 at https://store.samhsa.gov/system/files/sma14-4884.pdf.

van der Kolk, B. (2014) *The Body Keeps the Score: Brain, Mind, and Body in the Healing of Trauma.* New York, NY: Penguin.

Wang, M. T. and Kenny, S. (2014) 'Longitudinal links between fathers' and mothers' harsh verbal discipline and adolescents' conduct problems and depressive symptoms.' *Child Development 85*, 908–923.

Zehr, H. (2015) *Changing Lenses: Restorative Justice for Our Times* [Kindle version]. Harrisonburg, VA: Herald Press.

Appendix

DATE: . . . .   SCHOOL: . . . .

TRAUMA-INFORMED RESTORATIVE PRACTICES (RP) CHECKLIST

Please assess your school on each element according to the following scale:

1. Element is NOT AT ALL in place.

2. Element is PARTIALLY in place.

3. Element is MOSTLY in place.

4. Element is FULLY in place.

Please reflect on the trauma-informed restorative practices of your school and how they compare to the following draft district-wide characteristics. Use your assessment to identify top implementation priorities for your school.

Overall School Climate		
Rating	**RP look like/sound like/feel like**	**Comments**
1 2 3 4	Parents are aware of and have ownership of trauma-informed Restorative Justice in the school community.	
1 2 3 4	Students are aware of and have ownership of trauma-informed Restorative Justice in the school community.	
1 2 3 4	All staff across the school are aware of and have ownership of trauma-informed Restorative Justice in the school community.	
1 2 3 4	Clear and consistent processes exist to welcome new members (staff, students, and parents) into the community ("Entry Process").	
1 2 3 4	"Sense of Belonging" or Relational Ecology is tracked as a metric for all levels (admin, staff, students, parents).	
1 2 3 4	Every student is connected with an adult in the building for supports and goal-setting, and meets with that adult as least twice per week.	
	Circles (including student-led) are used regularly as a tool for:	
1 2 3 4	• community-building and social-emotional learning	
1 2 3 4	• critical incidents (loss of student or staff, student arrest, violent fights, lock downs, witnessing of fights)	
1 2 3 4	• academic circles	
1 2 3 4	• repairing harm	
1 2 3 4	• re-entry	
1 2 3 4	• parent involvement	
1 2 3 4	• staff and team meetings.	

1 2 3 4 **1 2 3 4** **1 2 3 4** **1 2 3 4** **1 2 3 4**	School climate is both trauma-informed and trauma-responsive: • All staff, students, and parents are trauma-informed. • Focus on co-regulation of staff, student, and parent stress factors. • All staff are aware of their own adverse childhood experiences (ACE) score. • Stress management is a foundational practice of the school culture for both students and staff. • A process is in place to identify and refer students of concern.
1 2 3 4 **1 2 3 4** **1 2 3 4** **1 2 3 4**	Equity has been a consideration in policy, climate and culture, and school discipline procedures: • Students and staff are aware of issues surrounding power, privilege, and oppression. • Dress codes are inclusive. • Considerations/ accommodations have been made for non-gender-conforming students to access restrooms. • RP take language barriers into consideration.
1 2 3 4	Mindfulness and socio-emotional learning are recognized as vital practices interwoven into all curricula.
1 2 3 4	Students are greeted by staff as they come into the building each morning. Students of concern are flagged for check-ins.

cont.

Overall School Climate		
Rating	**RP look like/sound like/feel like**	**Comments**
1 2 3 4 1 2 3 4 1 2 3 4	Respect agreements are living documents with frequent engagement: • in classrooms • between staff and admin; staff and staff • with parents as a tool for engagement.	
1 2 3 4	School contains predictable and safe environments (including classrooms, hallways, playgrounds, and school bus) that are attentive to transitions and sensory needs.	
1 2 3 4	Ongoing partnerships exist with state and community agencies to facilitate access to resources, including mental health and basic needs (access to counseling, food, resources, snacks, backpack programs, food pantry).	
1 2 3 4 1 2 3 4 1 2 3 4 1 2 3 4 1 2 3 4 1 2 3 4	Restorative dialogue exists between: • admin and teacher/staff/parents • admin and student • teacher/staff and teacher/staff • teacher/staff and student • student and student • parents and admin-staff.	
1 2 3 4 1 2 3 4 1 2 3 4	Community events in place to facilitate connections and sense of belonging (community-building) include: • non-school-based community • incoming students • pep rally.	
1 2 3 4	A buddy system or support system exists for teachers and staff.	

1 2 3 4	Visible symbols of community are in place (e.g., posters, worry stones, climate-positive visuals that reflect empowerment for all student identities, posters promoting Restorative Justice/RP).	

Discipline

1 2 3 4	RP exist in place of or in partnership with suspensions/detentions.	
1 2 3 4	Discipline policies are culturally and racially informed and trauma-responsive, including dress code, substance use, bullying.	
1 2 3 4	Clear and consistent process exists to welcome students who have been excluded from the community back to the community ("re-entry process").	
1 2 3 4	Crisis intervention plans and teams are in place with connections to the appropriate human service agencies and community partners, including mental health, police, and community health.	
1 2 3 4	Enhanced referral documentation forms reflect RP considerations.	
1 2 3 4	Calm rooms with trained staff are available and utilized as alternatives to suspensions and detentions with a focus on regulating student stress and reflecting on behaviors (e.g., re-direction room, Zen Room, mindfulness room, relaxation room).	
1 2 3 4	An RP process is established for regular check-ins with "at-risk" and/or students of concern.	

cont.

Discipline		
Rating	RP look like/sound like/feel like	Comments
1 2 3 4	"Community connection form" or circle request form is in place to enable members of the community to request circle discussions to build and/or repair relationships.	
1 2 3 4	Assessment of Lagging Skills and Unsolved Problems (ALSUP) is in place, and Plan B is used with students frequently involved with the discipline system.	
1 2 3 4	Peer mediation/peer monitoring/ youth court/youth panel is in place. Panel is youth-led.	
Restorative Justice/RP Implementation		
1 2 3 4	Development of climate specialist or Restorative Justice coordinator. Their role is clarified and clear with all parents, students, and staff.	
1 2 3 4	Support for staff is available on a regular basis, including supervision and/or consultation with a trauma expert, Restorative Justice consultant, as well as classroom observations, and opportunities for team work.	
1 2 3 4	Advisory curriculum reflects RP, including student training in RP (i.e., how to solve problems, be accountable, and repair harm one might cause).	
1 2 3 4	An RP-trained person is available during the day to assist (e.g., "circle keepers").	

1 2 3 4	"Upstanders" are recognized throughout the school (students and staff).
1 2 3 4	Implementation team of at least ten people is in place with admin leadership and support as well as parent involvement.
1 2 3 4	Implementation team meets on a regular basis (suggested twice a month).
	Ongoing training for staff exists to address the following topics:
1 2 3 4	• Nonviolent Communication™
1 2 3 4	• Collaborative and Proactive Solutions™
1 2 3 4	• the Five Skills of Restorative
1 2 3 4	• circle training
1 2 3 4	• mindfulness
1 2 3 4	• equity in education
1 2 3 4	• trauma-informed classrooms, including de-escalation, ACEs, and resilience
1 2 3 4	• refreshers on core beliefs
1 2 3 4	• staff-wide calibrations
1 2 3 4	• student-led and teacher-led training.

RP CHECKLIST—SCHOOL-SPECIFIC PRIORITIES

Based on your checklist results above, please list your top 5 priorities and indicate related time frames to address (these items can then be reflected in your school's RP plan).

Priority	Action(s) to Address	Time Frame

This document is the product of collaboration between the Restorative Justice Implementation teams at Meriden Public Schools, Hartford Public Schools, and Joe Brummer Consulting, LLC. For more information, contact: www.joebrummer.com

Index

Page numbers followed by lower case *t* or *f* indicate tables and figures respectively. Footnotes are indicated with n followed by the footnote number.